FOL
. 50

D0444913

ACTION

ACTION

A BOOK ABOUT SEX

Amy Rose Spiegel

GRAND CENTRAL
PUBLISHING

NEW YORK   BOSTON

The names and identities of romantic partners in the book have been changed.

Copyright © 2016 Amy Rose Spiegel

Cover design by Elizabeth Turner
Cover copyright © 2016 by Hachette Book Group, Inc.

All rights reserved. In accordance with the U.S. Copyright Act of 1976, the scanning, uploading, and electronic sharing of any part of this book without the permission of the publisher constitute unlawful piracy and theft of the author's intellectual property. If you would like to use material from the book (other than for review purposes), prior written permission must be obtained by contacting the publisher at permissions@hbgusa.com. Thank you for your support of the author's rights.

Grand Central Publishing
Hachette Book Group
1290 Avenue of the Americas
New York, NY 10104

grandcentralpublishing.com
twitter.com/grandcentralpub

First Edition: May 2016

Grand Central Publishing is a division of Hachette Book Group, Inc.
The Grand Central Publishing name and logo is a trademark of
Hachette Book Group, Inc.

The Hachette Speakers Bureau provides a wide range of authors for speaking events. To find out more, go to www.hachettespeakersbureau.com or call (866) 376-6591.

The publisher is not responsible for websites (or their content) that are not owned by the publisher.

Library of Congress Cataloging-in-Publication Data

Names: Spiegel, Amy Rose, author.
Title: Action : a book about sex / Amy Rose Spiegel.
Description: First edition. | New York : Grand Central Publishing, 2016. | Includes index.
Identifiers: LCCN 2015050562| ISBN 978-1-4555-3449-4 (paperback) | ISBN 978-1-478-96077-5 (audio download) | ISBN 978-1-4555-3450-0 (ebook)
Subjects: LCSH: Sex. | Sexual excitement. | Sexual intercourse. | Sex instruction. | BISAC: SELF-HELP / Personal Growth / Happiness. | SELF-HELP / Personal Growth / Self-Esteem. | SELF-HELP / Sexual Instruction. | HUMOR / General.
Classification: LCC HQ31 .S745 2016| DDC 306.7—dc23 LC record available at http://lccn.loc.gov/2015050562

Printed in the United States of America

RRD-C

10 9 8 7 6 5 4 3 2 1

For you/yes/you

Contents

Introduction   *xi*

PART I

Age of Consent   3

Gender, Neutrally   13

Boy About Town   16

Alone in the Bone Zone   19

Become Yourself   23

From the Inside Out   38

Introducing Everyone   45

No, I Still Want to Lick a Face from the Web   54

Whom Should You Bone?   60

Some Notes on Grooming   63

PART II

Protect Me from What I Want   83

In the Act   100

PART III

Mistakes Were Made   181

The Case for Celibacy   193

On Sluts   197

Further Resources   207

Acknowledgments   209

Index   211

Dilige et quod vis fac.

Love, and do what you will.

—*Confessions*, St. Augustine of Hippo

Introduction

Love and do what you will is the only inflexible truth I can tether myself to, belief-wise. Restated, it means: *Be kind, and you can't be wrong.* Another of Augustine's life-defining ideas to which I fervidly subscribe: the pursuit of sex, which he famously prioritized in his life—and felt mad conflicted about. Augustine's tail-chasing career was truncated when he buckled to contrary opinions held by his religion about what sort of behavior qualified as "holy" (turns out boning is pretty much the opposite of Christian divinity, in their literal book), but I think he was right the first time around. One can absolutely treat sex as a conduit for connectivity with the world.

Biologically, we are configured to want and be with one another. Sex accounts for such a sprawling part of what I consider sacramental because it's also the hardware of my genetics. Sex is high and low: the nexus of culture-shaping religious rites, elemental science, and the visual motif of a lot of the best music videos as yet committed to the canon. I notice how it structures the highs and lows of my life, too, and how that framework overlaps—or not—with other people's blueprints—and whether I should totally bone them, if our schematics work together interestingly.

Every person I sleep with is a new machine, albeit one with the same set of instructions: *Be loving in a new way. Love like you did not know how to love before.* My sexual partners each show me new forms of communicating Augustine's kindness, the most airtight definition of love that I know.

This is *not* to say that I'm conflating sex and love. HA, can you imagine? You'd close the book here, like, "No thanks—I think we're *alllll* set for today," and you'd be right. But I *do* clock private information about a person from the way they have sex. Seeing and becoming involved with someone in a fuck-based capacity evinces new things about them—and about me—even if those truths are only true right then and there, and neither of us ever have a similar experience again. Personal details pertaining to sex are not necessarily *secret*, but they're usually more clandestine than most other biographical compositions, and I feel lucky whenever anybody lets me in on theirs. Even in the most easygoing arrangements, a person who is undressed in a bedroom (or wherever) is vulnerable, physically and psychically. They are also redolent with a specific kind of power, *and*, I hope, about to have a hell of a lot of fun.

A lot of the time, I have sex in order to see what's possible—to become an updated version of the person I thought I was. I want to traverse as much as I can of the unending range of what I and other people are capable of enjoying (together). I love having sex with someone if I can feel that we're changing together—beyond the basic "marching ever closer to hanging out with the Grim Reaper" parade. (Isn't that the point of the processional?) These alterations can be small—as in, *I have never slotted a hand down the pants of this particular personage, at this particular date and time, before RIGHT THIS INSTANT! Man, I am ALL-NEW!* In other cases, they've felt more revelatory, like, *Whoa, I guess I love sleeping with women, when I did not suspect that to be the case previously!* Becoming ALL-NEW does not mean that anything you do is reflective on any part of your overarching *identity in life*—unless you want it to be. In the moment, you are still *you*, regardless of what you do. Imposing broad, uncritical rules on sex rankles me—*this is right; this is wrong.* I prefer to think, Yo! *This is possible? Fascinating!* (And then maybe fantasize about it later, if the memory of it rustles up that impulse.)

I love talking and thinking about sex as much as I do having it. Speaking about sex comes, in part, from the attendant preference for wanting to listen to how others feel about it, too. In this book I have tried not to mistranslate and express ownership over experiences that are not mine, which is exactly the behavior that leaves people feeling overlooked, erased from the record, and socially shut down. All I can do is recount how sex has featured in my life and how that has felt. I'm not a doctor—I am equipped to write about sex only in that I am a person who has a pretty normal life that (mostly) does not include anxiety meltdowns about sex i/r/t identity. If I am "qualified" to be honest about my whole sexual deal, of course you are, too. No academic degree—or degree of skankitude—can imbue someone with the grand and lofty ability to know what feels good for them/fuck like a maniac; you've already got that (if you want it).

I am trying not only to talk about sex, but also putting forth mad ideas about how to get your partners to talk back (remember that whole fun "listening" gambit? It pays off!). I am a single person, albeit one who happens to have been with many others, so this book cannot even come close to encompassing the boundless interactions people have with their partners. (I'm wild grateful for that—homogeneity is boring, and premature death.) I do not expect you to agree with me throughout all of this. I'd rather you observe the aspects in which you are unlike me—and make up your own mind about how *you'd* have met the decisions I came to.

This is ostensibly a contemporary, youthful, we-do-it-so-different-here's-how-we're-special-and-new guide to the rutting that our ancestors have enjoyed and started wars over since humankind took its place among the cosmic junk of our vast and terrible universe, so I'll quickly hearken back to my original point.

Here is what you learn about a person when you're taking off their clothes: Are they good to the people they fuck—those people in those vulnerable, powerful states of anticipatory pleasure, trust, and fear? Yo—are *you*?

You are, and you can show them how to be good to you. (And have great orgasms about it.) I think we're about ready to figure out how that goes down. *Dilige et quod vis fac.* Let's go get some action.

By Definition: A Glossary of Terms

asexual: Used to describe a person who does not experience, or feel compelled to act on, sexual desire.

cis and cisgender: Used to describe a person whose male or female gender identity is the one widely expected of the body they were born with.

non-binary: Someone whose male or female gender identity, or attraction to partners, does not adhere tightly to the one expected of them or the people to whom they are attracted.

person with a penis/vagina; "they" vs. "she"/"he" pronouns: For the sake of simplicity, and with as much of an eye toward gender neutrality as I could manage without muddling the text, I am using the pronouns "he" and "she" to correspond to diction in which I would have preferred to use "the person with the penis," "the person with the vagina," or "they." I had to make a decision about clarity, and I apologize to readers whose bodies don't correspond precisely with the pronoun that I've used at any point. I thought about this throughout every step of writing this book and have tried to be inclusive while bearing this in mind, but I have only one set of experiences, and it would be really gross if I tried to subvert or circumvent that fact by pretending otherwise. I hope you can find something of value here, despite any discrepancies of language.

rape culture: A society that blames and tries to shame a victim of rape and does not properly prosecute or socially condemn the criminals who commit it, regardless of whether the law states that rape is a crime. Also, a society that normalizes the sexual degradation of women.

rape/sexual assault: Not just forced penetration. Any sexual act that is committed without the clear permission of all parties involved.

sex: "Sex" is not necessarily a synonym for "intercourse"— or any other act that involves skin-on-skin contact. A working definition: *Sex* can be whatever act fills in the gaps between any number of bodies, which of course includes—and can even extend exclusively to—the brains operating them. Some people prefer to cultivate their sex lives in solitude. Although the majority of non-asexual people partner up at some point or another, plenty of your fellow humans don't engage in double-sided physical sexuality. Others are down to mess around with another person only if a phone or computer is mediating the distance between them.

Nontraditional sexual methods are as much about negotiating the space around a body as any in-the-flesh arrangement. Sex takes the shape of its container, meaning it can adapt to whatever vessel your body and brain decide for it. So: Yes, it means vaginal or anal penetration. But it also means basically whatever you want it to.

sex-positive: A term that I really loathe and try to avoid, as it makes me feel like somebody's beatific aunt who uses an "alternative" form of deodorant. Still I can appreciate the impetus behind "sex positive." It connotes that something or someone is frank, open, friendly, and communicative about sex, that they see and recognize all genders as equal, and that it doesn't have to be a seedy, morally repugnant secret if you are titillated by bodies (or most of the other things a person can be turned on by).

My distaste is not only about the intense "key party" atmosphere around *sex-positive*—I also don't like the term because differentiating a healthy and normal attitude toward sex by bestowing it with a special title reinforces that mindset as marginal while holding up that the "normal" thing is to revile sex, which I earnestly do not think most people do. Despite its faults, "sex-positive" will help you find sex stores, literature, and pornography that make more sense to you than a lot of mainstream kinds, in many cases. You won't catch it in this book, though—at least not without audible groaning.

sex versus gender: Your sex is what a doctor decided based on what they saw between your legs on your zeroth birthday and then wrote a letter on a certificate. Your gender is "male," "female," and/or any designation between or outside those roles that you feel most closely matches the person you are in a way that extends to the rest of your body and mind.

PART I

Age of Consent

The number one most essential part of any and all sexual encounters: establishing the often-hazy-seeming-but-actually-pretty-clear parameters of "consensual sex," which is otherwise known as "sex." Sexual consent is a direct verbal go-ahead that conveys, "What we're doing with our bodies is okay with me," as confirmed before *not only* sex involving penetration, but *so many other* kinds of sensual scenarios, too. Consent is an important part of getting down with anybody, of any gender or sexual persuasion, every single time you're getting down. In fact, it's probably *the* most important part: If you're in a physical situation where the other person disregards that you've told them not to touch you in the way they're touching you, what you're experiencing isn't sex (a catchall term I'm using here for "hookups of all stripes"), but sexual assault, and possibly rape. There is a plethora of ways to give and receive consent—and to refuse it. We'll explore as many of them as we can here today. Is that okay with you? (Look! We've already begun. I wish it were always this easy.)

While it may seem obvious that consent extends to far more than "Can I sexually freaq your bod now, or . . . ?" too many of us have been with people who don't understand that getting prior clearance can be as necessary for relatively low-impact activities, like kissing, as it is for sexual bod-freaqing. In moments spent with those types of people, the inside of my younger brain mostly neurosis'd out thusly: *Wait, what the literal heck, I thought this person LIKED ME, so WHY IS HE TRYING TO HARASS MY LAP OUT OF NOWHERE, do I go along with this weird crotch-vasion or risk losing his company forever??? Can we just go back* to *thinking that biting each other's lips was the most torrid this was going to get, please? Plus, am I strong enough to overpower him if I have to?* This is not what the internal monologue of a person given over to erotic ecstasy sounds like, Alex-from-the-bar-on-the-corner-whom-I-made-out-with-because-I-was-bored! Thanks for the panic attack!

When someone instigates sexual contact that you haven't agreed to, it can be tough to negotiate how to feel—let alone what to do. First of all, that's totally normal, and second of all, it has got to change, because I want you to have fulfilling, electrifyingly hot encounters *of the flesh* (ew, this lasciviously horrible turn of phrase) without feeling pressured, uncomfortable, or, heaven forbid, endangered along the way. *Or* like you're some kind of frumped-out killjoy for simply saying no, because YOU AREN'T. *Orrrrr* like you can't have rough sex AND non-negotiable boundaries at the same time. You know better than anyone else what feels good and manageable to you and what doesn't. (And this would be true *even if* Mark Ruffalo somehow merged with Sappho into a single, sexually masterful entity, and that being sidled up to you all like, "...Hhhhello there, allow me to playfully lick you on the forearm, my dove.") You have the absolute right to broadcast these non-negotiable preferences to every individual to whom you decide to affix your various and sundry (and sultry, *my dove*) body parts. No lap-harassment or weird crotchvasions necessary. Unless that's what you're into.

On the whole, my bod-freaqing, et cetera, has been wild enjoyable. (I *know*, I am a *very* cool sex-haver, CHECK OUT MY COOL-GUY HAIRSTYLE AND STYLISH DENIM JEANS.) I've also had some less-than-sterling, and occasionally downright awful, experiences with partners who didn't seem to consider whether I was all right with what was happening between us—and there have definitely been times when *I* was too pushy, and we'll talk about all of these occasions in a little. First, though, an abridged list of illustrative quotations from *Remembrances of Bone Zones Past* (RoBZP), my mental encyclopedia of belt notches (this is *not* to be confused with Proust's classic literary masterpiece, which was definitely at high risk of happening here):

- "I didn't think you wanted me to use a condom."
- "Just relax. You'll like it."
- "You were okay with it last time."
- "I forgot you weren't into that."
- "This is the only way it feels good for me."

All of these are real-life garbage sentences, uttered by real-life garbage people in response to my protestations about some dubious piece of the "action" we were getting. Sometimes these people were also actual rapists (because, straight-up, anyone who disregards your not wanting to have sex, or coerces you into it after you say no, fits this description). Though these phrases were deployed in different scenarios/for ostensibly different reasons, each one means, "I don't care what you want, even though you just directly told me that *it isn't what is happening*, and I don't respect you as a person more than I do my own horniness in this one moment."

To operate under that mindset when someone has trusted you with the privilege of feeling all up on them is *wholly unacceptable*, and not only because you're trying to make that person feel bad for your own repugnant behavior. (Not, you know, "you," but some hypothetical Alex-from-next-to-the-jukebox-style garbaggio-fuck, whom I'm now itching to destroy in vengeance of your honor even though he's technically made up.) Any person who exercises this selfishness has bought into the set of false promises made to them by male-violence-dominated societies, aka that victims of sexual assault are responsible at least in part for the harm done to them, so the aggressors don't have to feel like it's their fault. This is untrue putrescence.

I know *you* (real you, this time) wouldn't be the kind of solipsistic cretin who thinks that way, but if you find yourself in a situation where someone is reciting a passage that sounds plagiarized from one of the above excerpts from the *RoBZP*, please understand that your decisions are sound and worth respecting, even though said scum is trying to make you feel guilty about the fact that they've decided it's okay for you to feel unhappy/uncomfortable/unsafe as long as they're feeling sexual pleasure. The idea of even the potential of that happening to you makes me want to mail a congressperson a stink bomb and yell obscene, hideous things at a beautiful phenomenon of nature—ideally a canyon, but definitely a majestic, centuries-old sycamore, *at least* (in addition to my previous crimes against fictional "Alex"-type pred-nesses).

You are entirely within your rights to let anyone trying to pull that know that they are acting execrably and extricate yourself from the scene immediately. In some terrible, wrenching situations, this self-removal is not an option for the person on whom sex is being pushed, as I also know firsthand. (I have no quips about my experience this time. It was just awful and that's it.) As we know, despite coming up in a social environment that doggedly tries to convince us of the opposite in order to keep traumatic physical harm a normal: Rape and sexual assault are never caused by their victim's behavior. They are the result of another person's callousness, and there is nothing you can do in this life to "deserve" or "invite" rape or sexual assault. The people on whom these acts are inflicted are sometimes led to believe that if they had somehow conducted themselves more responsibly and/or advocated for themselves more insistently, everything would have been A-OK. This is the highest caliber of cold bullshit. Even if you were drunk or on drugs. Another forever-true side note: You are entirely within your rights to stop fooling around with somebody if you're no longer into it, regardless of how considerate the other person is being. You don't need a reason or an excuse to not want to get with somebody, and you don't owe anyone a goddamn thing in that respect, ever. No one has a claim on your body but you.

I don't want to scare you off forever—most people are not angling to trap one another in these kinds of scenarios, but, if we're going to have this consent-versation, we have to acknowledge the fact that consent, though essential, is fallible. I think the gigantic, looming threat of potentially messing up when it comes to consent, and then being forever after labeled an abuser, assailant, or rapist, is part of why some members of the genuinely non-monstrous majority population are afraid to discuss it—and are, as a result, more likely to mess it up. (This is a shame, since verbally consensual sex is good, healthy, and the crowd favorite among highly skilled, hot, and respectful hookup candidates. I've had myriad physical experiences with well-meaning, resolutely decent types who just didn't seem to know how to address consent in a proactive and sexy way in the heat of the moment. As I mentioned, I have also been this species of person! I don't think everyone who stumbles when it comes to discussing consent is a rapist/predatory beast—many of them have never been made to understand that rape and sexual assault are things they even have to think about committing, since they are convinced that "rape" is a terrible act with just one meaning that *of course* would never be demonstrated by them. (I exhort these people to get an inch of a clue.) Others don't know how to bring up consent without getting skittish, feeling prim, worrying they're killing some kind of moment/boner/wide-on, or otherwise shutting down. This makes me sad, because avoiding consent because it's an "uncomfortable" topic actually steers people into the exact awkwardness they're trying to avoid: It leads to situations where two amenable foxes who set out to have a great time together end up snarled in a morass of anxiety, which is, at least from the maps I've drawn up in the front covers of *RoBZP* (as one does with fantasy novels) not usually their intended destination. It sincerely doesn't have to go down like that—in most cases, it is so easy for it NOT to go down like that! You just have to give each other directions.

At its best, sex, or making out, or touching regions, or whatever affectionate physical contact you're enjoying with another willing individual, is communicative and instructive in tons of ways. Every person has their own motions, methods, preferences, and modes when it comes to all these exercises. Learning

someone's personal specificities—and having them learn yours—
is edifying and sexy and worthwhile. One important condition on
which this is predicated, though, is mutual honesty and consideration, which—guess what—come from mutual consent.

I don't mean you have to permanently chuck spontaneity into
the garbage disposal mid-hookup to instigate a heart-to-pelvis
conversation about your entire sexual history and interior life
(although if that's what you need to do to feel comfortable about
being physical with another person, do it right up without a second
thought). But no matter how free 'n' breezy (or otherwise reminiscent of a feminine hygiene–centric commercial) your encounter,
you still have to pay attention to and interpret signals, respond to
cues, and intermittently ask questions. Those are the basics (but,
trust your girl, we'll delve deeper in just a moment). Speaking up
is so much easier—and so much more effective—than wordlessly
removing someone's hand from a part of your body where you'd
rather it not be fluttering around, although, frankly, your partner
should get the message from that alone.

Sex, for all its virtues, is weird (which is also frequently one
of its virtues). It can be hard to know what another person likes,
wants, or is thinking, or whether they're able to gauge what *you*
like, want, or are thinking without an explicit, out-loud announce-
ment from you...or vice versa: Treating your partners like pas-
sive sexual objects is not only insulting and wrongheaded, but
also overlooks the reality that it's crucial to ask the same consent-
based questions you require of them. Once you get into the habit
of putting words to that murky stuff, it'll be a massive relief and,
as a result, a more enjoyable, less intimidating headspace in which
to go about goin' at it.

The first tenet of consent: Each "yes" you give expires after a
single use. Since you are a person with mutable feelings, you might
want to do something one day, with one person, in one setting, but
you're not bound to those feelings forever. Giving some babe permission to come aboard your areas on one occasion doesn't give
aforementioned babe license to nonchalantly assume he/she/they

have clearance to do so forever after, or even just the next time around, (if there is one). You are not being unreasonable or prudish if you decide to draw the line or otherwise change your mind.

So, since you're going to be giving a LOT of it, it's time we delve into some specific ideas about *how* to grant someone consent—and how to decisively withhold it. The ideal time to talk about what your sexual limitations are: prior to becoming embroiled in a physical situation where someone might be straining them. If you're able to have a conversation with the person you're potentially going to be intimate with before acting on whatever that means for you, you can tell them exactly what you do/don't want to do. When I started seeing one long-term boyfriend, we spent a lot of time talking before anything beyond entry-level kissing took place between us, and while most of that conversation probably concerned our differences of opinion about what the best episode of *The Simpsons* was, we also asked each other plenty of questions about where to pause and check our sexual mile-marking systems to see if we were on the right track. Our answers were given candidly: I told him that at the time, I was inclined to wait a bit longer before having sex, among some other things that seemed intense to me. In turn, he told me about his history with sexual trauma, which made me rethink being too rough with him in ways I would have otherwise thought were playful when we actually started *going far* together. We knew each other's deals, and we didn't try to abruptly broker new ones mid-hookup without first considering them aloud while wearing clothing. Learning to ask and respond honestly to the question, "Do you want to try [whatever new thing]?" then actually taking heed of what was said, was probably what made the sex we had after a few months so brain-dominatingly incredible—we were both stoked and comfortable—and faithfully aware that the other person was, too. We still had our Milhouse–based differences, but all the other important approaches to compatibility, we agreed on.

Not every sexual situation is going to come out of a relationship. Though that one was awesome while it lasted, I also find that, *Whoa, so is attaching my face to people whose middle, or even last, names I don't know!* Those experiences proved the plentitude of frank, direct, flirtatious, and gentle ways to make consent a part of every hookup, regardless of how well you might (not) be acquainted. How you decide to approach the babes of your consensual and highly sexy future is up to you, but here are some pointers on how to score and feel great about it, how to make sure dreamboats-to-come are equally jazzed about what's going on, and what to do if things take a too-intense turn and you want to set them back on track.

If someone is coming on a bit strong for your tastes (how you determine this is, as with most things related to sex, subjective), tell them to alter what they're doing, or to stop, if you prefer. If you're all right with the former, pull away by a few inches and say something like "Do that [more slowly, or gently, or however you'd like them to change it], please." No matter what that directive is, don't couch it in language like "I don't think I want to do that yet" if you're *sure* you don't want to do that yet. You don't have to water down what you know in your heart/parts to be true, and your boundaries are not up for renegotiation unless you say, and mean, that they are.

In one of my frenches of yore, nothing much was "happening" that wasn't kissing, on the surface, but the Francophile in question had me pressed up against a wall and I wasn't into it, even though I was otherwise enjoying making out with her. Getting specific about what wasn't working for me righted that weirdness: "Hey, can you back up a little?" goes a long way, and not in the sexually figurative sense. She got the message that I wanted to SLOW RIDE, TAKE IT EASY in that instance, although we had hooked up in rough, restrictive, and generally raunch-as-hell ways before. When others have rammed their tongues down my esophagus, which has happened a solid throatful of times in my life, saying, "Can you be gentler, please?" has been similarly effective.

If you say, "I like it when you slow down," and then that person doesn't, I advise you to bail—and this advice extends to all kinds of sexual contact. First and most important: Physically separate yourself from this person, since your safety comes first, regardless of whatever they're doing to imply the contrary. Then, if you feel comfortable doing so, let them know why you're bailing. They should be aware that their supremely jerk-esque behavior is the reason they're about to be alone. Then, unless you have anything more you'd like to say, just leave.

Consent includes accounting for and protecting your physical health. You should always use some kind of barrier method that prevents STIs, like a condom, if you're having sex without also looking to conceive a kiddo. To be extra-safe throughout your encounter, you should also periodically check to make sure that barrier method stays in place. People can be surprisingly and infuriatingly boneheaded about this! Once upon a night that started out promisingly, I caught someone I was with trying to remove a condom without telling me. What a nightmare, right? When he explained that he assumed I'd be "chill about it," I freaked. How dare anyone treat anyone else with complete disregard for their health or personhood—and then be an idiot bro who tries to project his grossness onto me BY USING THE WORD "CHILL" AS AN ADJECTIVE. Yo, I became a banshee. I fucking hate that guy, and I wish I could tell the world his name so that he could see exactly how *chill* I am.

On the other end of the consensual spectrum, a recent hookup asked me if I'd gotten the Gardasil shot (an HPV vaccine). This sounds a lot less charming than it was, but trust me! I was kissing this person for the first time, and, even though it was unclear whether things would go further, he wanted to let me know before they did that he carried the virus, so any decisions I made that evening would be informed ones. "That's admirable of you to tell me," I said, feeling a little too impressed. His response was even better: "It's not! I just think you have the right to know whether I could potentially be giving you something like that." That is exactly how to be! In case anyone tries to tell you that pausing an experience to ask questions, provide information, and/or make sure all of the proceedings are cool with your partner "kills the mood," let me tell you, his honesty made me like him even more, which is usually the case with any kind of sexual encounter—or every brand of life encounter. It doesn't make me want to have sex with a person *less* if they let me know they want me to like it, including after we split ways. That's just bad logic.

Sex, like any way of relating to another person, is at its very greatest when you and the cohort you've chosen to hang around with listen to each other and generally make a point of keeping kindness and respect at the forefronts of your minds. I know that part won't be hard for you. Even though hooking up with other people can be unpredictable, I hope you go into every situation knowing and trusting that whatever your sexual parameters are, they're exactly the right ones to work inside of. You know what you want—and so should anyone on the other end of whatever that means for you. Go get it.

Gender, Neutrally

Treating sex as an unsavory, improper, or inappropriate topic is one of the most oppressive forces grinding down our individual and collective happiness. You know how anything more revelatory than stony opacity about money—talking about one's salary, expenditures, et cetera—is considered gauche? Clock how the richest people continue to remain the only segment of the population with access to the wildly complex specifics of how becoming wealthy functionally happens while the poor are stuck with "secrets" that nobody wants to know and that everyone already knows anyway, aka that being broke sucks, life is too expensive, debt is meant to fuck you not help you, and money is everything.

Sex is similar, except in this case, the stigmatized are people who cop to being interested in it who aren't straight men. (And then straight men are left working inside a system where they are supposed to believe that they're the only people who enjoy, or are being served by, sex, which, in addition to being morally and ethically backward—plus interpersonally alienating—makes them garbage lays, and advises them to police some of the people they'd benefit from allowing sexual autonomy. All of that is far less pressing than what precedes this parenthetical, though.) The ettiquette in play here works the same way as shushing salary talk: things stay the same for those reaping the paver, and vice versa.

I suspect that many of our internal panic-hurricanes that keep us from talking about sex come from whether we're convincingly puppeteering the gendered costumes we're wearing—whether we know that that's the cause of our anxieties or not. As with so many of life's dumbest facets, shyness surrounding sex can stem in part from how masculine and feminine norms are expressed on a cultural level, which is to say *immaculately*. THEY'RE THE BEST, JUST LOVE 'EM, LUV BEING A "GIRL" WITH MY "PURSE" OF "HAIRSTYLES."

No, of course gender roles necessitate feelings of inadequacy in their very being. That is their point. It's absurd, but who among us hasn't felt like shit based on observing the twinkling heteronormatoné casts of toothpaste commercials, or by uneasily taking in comedy routines about the uproarious and irreconcilable differences between the sexes as conveyed by our attitudes about Valentine's Day/parents-in-law/the color or yeastiness of the alcoholic beverages we like (followed by the equally boring commentary about just how *downright condemnable* those aforementioned yuk-yuk jokes are for assuming broad tropes of nuanced people— aka this sentence)? We are made to feel rude for our difference.

Unfortunately, we have to keep talking about the particulars of how we're socialized to absorb and display the expectations for our genders. One of many cogent reasons: They're wrecking our sex lives. And if you think that seems trivial? (a) This may not be the book for you; and (b) consider every vicious politician who's ever sublimated his terror that liking a finger in an orifice means he's GAY into a law that kills or maligns or otherwise tries to place a harness on the population writ large, then maybe get back to me. I'll be right here, combing my beautiful female handbag as I wince back my anger, just like I'm supposed to!

Far more preferable, far more loving, far more honest, far fucking hotter: Asking for and paying attention to the User's Guide for how each of your specific partners wants to feel good and checking that information against whether their proclivities dovetail with what it is that does it for you—and not making your bedfellows feel ashamed about the things they like and want that you're not down to try out with them. Having as many (or as few!) orgasms as you want, with whomever you want, as long as everyone involved is okay with that. Seeing all of what the world can give you and the other way around: Filling your dance card with other living, thinking, boning beings before you go check out the afterlife. (Freud describes sex, or *eros*, as the "life instinct" that human beings use to combat Thanatos, or the underlying knowledge, in all things, of the reality that we're all going to kick one day.) Doing all the weird shit you search for on the internet—and doing it consensually. Most crucial: *talking about sex.* Not just in the beginning of whatever affair you might be having at the moment, but throughout and beyond the actual doing-of-it. You don't need to narrate every last gesture that takes place between you and a sexual attaché—once consent is in place, a lot of what's great about fucking, in the moment, is ineffable—but to treat it, more generally, as taboo is to stiffen and truncate its unknowns. You don't have to worry about whether that makes you "gay," or whatever, because that's up to you and only you to decide. Please stop voting otherwise, if you are.

In *The History of Sexuality*, the social theorist Michel Foucault lays out the concept of something called "repressive hypothesis." This is, paraphrased simply, the idea that in saying, "Our society is so prim and uptight about sex!" we reinforce that taboo, when we could be ameliorating the tension by just talking about the thing itself—sex!—instead (and of course having sex). Attempting to skew the acknowledgment of sexual repression and its attendant hang-ups into "social progression" does nothing to improve our shared situation, because we're not saying anything productive or meaningful about the ways we fuck. Instead, we're strengthening the lack of permissiveness we're bemoaning by catering to it. We can be smarter than that. Plus, talking about sex is a guaranteed-to-be-entertaining pastime, if literally all of television, film, literature, and sitting on the passenger side of my sister's car are any indication. I honestly can't see what's rude about that.

Boy About Town

I don't have a sexual "orientation."

My personal theme song is by a band called, fittingly, the Jam. There are many reasons why I love "Boy About Town," outside of the sole fact that it's a through-and-through life-affirmer, quality-wise. It tracks a young ruffian who's on the move:

> See me walking around, I'm the boy about town that you heard of.
> See me walking the streets, I'm on top of the world that you heard of.

The sunny hustle mapped out by the lyrics matches the daily flânerie of my thinking—scattershot, blithe, far-flung: *Oh, like paper caught in wind, I glide upstreet, I glide downstreet*. Like a raffish prettyboy traipsing through life with all the pride and beauty of itinerant trash picked up by a breeze, I cruise.

In gay male culture, *cruising* signifies a casual process of selecting and catching onto a temporary sexual cohort—if a guy is *cruising*, he's testing the currents of all his potential sexual options, looking to see what strangers out there he might take home with him. That verb's meaning for all people, in a slightly different sense, is also the general shape of my attitudes and manner when I am feeling most like myself: I drift, I pass through easily, I shred along the pathways of my life delicately and with joy, I travel forth in a manner that's generally steady, if circuitous. I see how wide and sprawling the world is as though through a window of a plane that is cruising at 40,000 feet, and I am able to observe the interstellar-feeling smallness of its landscape's dappled towns and cities, each light a cosmos of faraway people, direction-inversion: *all those stars down there*. It feels something like this idea from Audre Lorde: "There's always someone asking you to underline one piece of yourself— whether it's Black, woman, mother, dyke, teacher, etc.—because that's the piece that they need to key in to. They want to dismiss everything else. But once you do that, then you've lost…Only by learning to live in harmony with your contradictions can you keep it all afloat." Hovering in this way, I feel like a spacecraft.

Part of that is shucking off any one orientation. I am not a lesbian. I am not straight, nor am I bisexual. Not identifying feels luxurious: It is professing the right to visit with each of the coruscating dots I admire as I travel, rather than deciding a single, fixed star as my home. While this works well for me, many people with more discrete gender identities and sexual proclivities have felt unmoored inside of communities of people unlike them for their whole lives, and so find great power, camaraderie, and newfound convenience re: finding boneable people, and other blessed benefits in identifying. After all, to "orient yourself" is to affix your meaning, and your place—a right from which non-straight, non-cis, and trans people have long been disallowed. You have a right to decide your own name—to settle into a home rather than take to the streets, or to the space between bodies.

Another line from the Jam's itinerant boy: *Oh, I'm sitting watching rainbows, and watching the people go crazy*. While aligning yourself with a specific sexual orientation can open you up to protection and love of all-new magnitudes, you can also move between homes when it comes to embodiments. I never designated myself "straight," or "gay," or "bisexual," depending on whom I was dating/fucking, because to do so made each of those words feel like the bigots who call fluctuating sexualities "faddish" were being thrown sturdy proof, even though that's bullshit and everyone has the right to claim whatever gender they like for themselves, even if they capitulate. But I did not know how to mean any of these things, and I felt bad for potentially skewing their definitions for the people who did. I wasn't doing anyone any harm, and it was fine for me to slip on identities as I felt them, but I prefer a mode that draws mainly on the fact that I can hook up with anyone I want, and it doesn't have to change what I *am*. I could call myself any one of those things, despite my dalliances outside of their normal confines, and be correct. I don't want to.

I have to say *something*. Otherwise, how would people know that they've got a shot with me, or that I had the wiring to scout them out? Here is as close as I can manage, as far as how a name for my gender identity and sexual orientation might sound: *queer*. I picture it as a spaceship, or, no—of course, a cruise ship. Picture one of the massive ocean liners in romantic comedies from the 1970s (coincidentally, my favorite aesthetic may be found among the streamers, muted pinks, and dinner gowns native to this decade's cinematic boats): I am uneasy when people confine me to a specific word when my heart feels as roomy and compartmented as a sea vessel. I am open to whatever kinds of aliens might want to float along on holiday with me.

To make it easier in my conversations and writing, "queer" is vague enough to wrap me up loosely, like a one-size-fits-all floral caftan (told you I was all about that *Love Boat* lifestyle). For the most part, I say, "I sleep with people of all genders." It does not make me feel like I'm obscuring my heart's actual shape with a free 'n' breezy muumuu-word. It does not put off someone who was trying to put it on me. "Queer" may not be "cruiser," but it is sufficient. And succinct enough to preserve the amount of time I would have taken explaining all of this in person, freeing me to spend it starfucking instead. While being a dilettante in terms of what gender your partners are doesn't have to dictate the way you identify—you can be a heterosexual man, make out with a guy, and have the first part of that status remain firmly true—I don't really care about any of it. I cruise forth.

Oh, please leave me aside, I want to be a...I want to be... I want to live in...There's more than you can hope for in this world.

Alone in the Bone Zone

Feeling sexy mostly has to do with YOU YOURSELF—with your inner foundation, regardless of whether another person's opinion of/attraction to that self sweeps through it. According to Dr. David Schnarch's book *Intimacy and Desire*: "A person's relationship to their self-worth likely informs their relationship to sex more so than lust, romantic love, and attachment. How you see yourself [...] profoundly shape[s] your sexual desire." So if you see yourself as an animate slime-filled trash bag, that correlates to the mucked-upness of the sex you're having (if you're even having it).

Even though I am not always a prime-feeling or -looking person, I try my best to conduct myself majestically, regardless of the times when I've been (or at least felt) overworked, poor, lonesome, ugly, anxious, depressed, and so forth. Shove yourself in front of the world, and become near-to-deranged with goodwill and hard work, and I promise: Gilding the kingdom of your brain will help you establish a "sex life" by building, first, a multilayered "life," no modifiers necessary.

Allow yourself to become flooded by your own personality, and make a concerted effort to get rid of the shame that allows you to muffle it for other people's "comfort." Most of the time, you're not *comforting* anyone by editing yourself; you're reinforcing that there is one right picture of how to be in the world, and that it likely does not resemble the one that comes to *others* naturally, too.

You know how everyone wanted to make out with David Bowie? His specificity, and his exacting dedication to presenting the world with the person he was rather than the ideal of what other people might think is "sexy" or "masculine" or "human, in any sense" is why we were convinced he was so good-looking. (Well, that and his hypercolor eyes.)

The sex-symbolization of a man who willfully tried to pass as an extraterrestrial among us earthlings imparts a cogent lesson: Be and look like *you*, and do not make a single apology, unless being deferential is a natural and crucial part of that you-ness. Confidence in the character and appearance you've got is not only the most attractive thing going, save for an unclassifiable eye color, but also the most *comforting* to others—it's signing a permission slip allowing them to surface their idiosyncrasies, too. Consider how people always try to make comedians laugh: They're attempting to exchange the social currency they think professional stand-ups find most valuable (usually while telling really bad jokes). If what, in your actions, you prove is valuable to you is unique strange foxadociousness, you will attract a trail of other unself-conscious foxes who've caught the scent of your freak pheromones. Besides, who wants to fuck a clod? OTHER CLODS, AND HOW THEY FIND THEM IS BY BEING CLODDISH. You are *not that clod*.

If you are positive in your belief that you are, in fact, the worst and least attractive person who ever slunk shamefacedly through the atmosphere—the anti-Bowie—there are a few ways to dodge that insecurity, which, I'll argue, is ultimately rather self-centered: I can say that with confidence, since, for a while, I couldn't bear to say ANYTHING with confidence, and when I let my insecurities monopolize me, it's the most I ever focus on MYSELF MYSELF MYSELF! When I quiet my life down because I'm afraid it looks funny otherwise, low self-esteem and narcissism deaden the air around me that other living beings could otherwise be deeply breathing in. Why would I do that, when, instead, I can go hunt for archival tour T-shirts at the thrift spot, or try to beat the old heads at chess in the park (never gonna happen), or get ten people I know haven't met one another, but would true-to-definitely like one another, together in a room? *No, I'd much rather stay here in bed, half-dressed, worrying that I'm inert, in large part because I am!!!* That's bad logic, plus solipsistic, plus a snore convention. You know who you are already, so whenever I'm picking myself apart, I remember that its more interesting to extend my hand out to someone else, regardless of who they are, to shake hello.

Of course you have to pay exclusive attention to yourself sometimes, but it's atrocious to think about yourself *all* the time, which is what you're up to if you're gazing at a Hope Diamond of a dime-piece and ruminating to the tune of, *I'm gonna screw up I always say something ungraceful I want to know and then french that person I won't be able to muster not zero of the nerve to go over there no way not never.* The proper amount of *you* in there, if we were to trim that thought-attack down to its one valid germ, is: *I want to know, and then french, that person.* Notice how the rest of it takes place in either the future or the past—and how the selected trimming is the sole part of the thought that accounts for a person outside yourself? That's the only current truth. The rest is YOURSELF YOURSELF YOURSELF, and not even your real self, but some fictitious version of you involved in events that aren't even going down to begin with. Do your best not to focus on that mirage self-portrait of a basket case to whom you bear little true resemblance, when you could be admiring the Hope Diamond.

So create an empire of your life and your for-real self—the person other people are waiting for you to present them with: the person who doesn't otherwise exist. Do, make, and enjoy excellent things. When you find yourself slinking around unattractively, you can call upon the memory that you just Jet-Skied through a glass ceiling, or made a Lego model of Seinfeld's apartment to scale, or learned a new chord progression on your sick-nasty electric keyboard. Or whatever it is you enjoy.

Even if some of this seems beyond reach—especially the part about commandeering a WaveRunner through the patriarchy—much more of it is eminently possible. And I feel lucky about that! I think often of something the cartoonist Chris Ware once said in an interview for *Rookie*, a publication for teenagers for which I am a story editor: "Being able to say 'I don't know what to do with my life' is an incredible privilege that 99 percent of the rest of the world will never enjoy."* I don't want to squander the arbitrary and overwhelming luck I have to be able to be and do and see all kinds of things and people! I have all this splendor in front of me. It would be a waste of my life to spend it sulking about how "unfuckable," and therefore unhappy, I am, when there's no causality there and neither have to be true.

Here's how to be a hot person, regardless of your externalities: *Stuff your life.* When you do: You'll find that you're not even doing it to attract somebody, once you get going, because the best thing to do with your life is everything (and also everyone). Look around for the kind of ideal company you're already keeping all by yourself. If you decorate your world, people will come to gawp admiringly at all of its many ornaments. In looking at the great fortune of your self-possession, others will be tempted to follow your example. (And also have sex with it.) You are *yourself*, and you are brimming.

---

* Tavi Gevinson, "Work Hard and Be Kind: An Interview with Chris Ware," *Rookie* magazine, Issue 15: Invention (2012), accessed 2015, http://www.rookiemag.com/2012/11/chris-ware-intervie/.

Become Yourself

Make borderline-severe eye contact with everyone. (And, while we're keeping it stodgily parental in this bit of advice, please: Sit up straight): Look right into the face of the person with whom you're yammering. Allow it to feel deliberate, but not invasive. In the most fledgling sexual/social capacity, like when you're encountering a babe for the very first time and are tempted instead to openly gawp at them, it's extra-important to be able to identify the difference between "flirtatious" and "intrusive/lecherous/looking for a pepper-spraydown": Is the other person willfully involved in conversation with you? You're golden. If they aren't, but they *are* looking back with pleasant interest/their tongue running across their teeth like YEAH YOU WANT THIS? you're *also* probably golden. If they look away and appear in any way bummed, HALT. You are initiating a staring contest with someone who'd rather not compete.

Some might be unsettled by prolonged eye-to-eye (does everyone else *also* have social anxiety?), but I promise almost all will thrill at being its recipient. Holding the gaze of someone with whom you're conversing (or would like to be) isn't awkward, as I once thought despite the urgings of every last cliché about making solid impressions. It's just good etiquette. But, like most overtures based in diligent manners, many people aren't used to it. Use this sense of novelty to highlight your own social rectitude: Letting a person speak with your eyes trained on theirs gives them the rare chance to feel heard when they're talking. Sensuous stare-downs are efficacious because, to many people, nothing is sexier than the feeling of being paid clear attention to. This is how Bill Clinton not only became president, but convinced the national masses of his charm, too—he is often said to make those he interacts with feel like the only person in a room, regardless of their politics. The first step in copying that magnetism is letting the person you're interested in know you can SEE them in said room, and that you find what you're looking at compelling enough to linger on it. There is enormous value in conveying that a person deserves—and downright commands—respectful, attentive interest, even if you end up getting nothing out of it.

Listen closely: Charisma isn't anything but the skillful delivery of focused attention. I have a rampant case of ADHD and still know better than to interrupt. Or maybe, because my brain is inclined to tug me in every direction at once, I have carefully practiced the great art of clamming up for a change. Pretend you have ADHD, I guess? Just don't extend that to neural drifting while someone speaks to you. Endeavor to hear them as though you'll be tested on the information later.

Unlike coursework: If you know squat about the material at hand, listening closely becomes even easier. The interests belonging to my past sexual partners that I thought were most captivatingly hot never coincided with my own. Oral histories of *anything* I've never previously been inclined to be curious about absolutely do it for me: I don't care much about clothes, but I was totally fascinated and charmed when one dude rhapsodized about the structures and colorways of classic sneakers. I maintain no grandiose passion for primatology, but the dude I saw who knew everything there was to know about chimpanzees was going to get smashed from the second he said the words "animal behaviorism." Encouraging people to talk about the things they care for most in the world is equitably rad for both parties—watch your orator's enthusiasm compound and compound as they motormouth their greatest loves at you. They seem equal parts blissed out, relaxed, engaged, and excited, right? *Hmm*...in which other kinds of interactions is that a totally advantageous state of mind? (Which is to say...*of bodyyy?*)

You are going to hella learn from the tiny colloquia people spout your way when you ask them what they think the best thing in the world is. Making people feel heard, as with making them feel seen, is valuable even if you don't score. You collect its primary benefit—personal edification—and then the added bonus of being able to offer it up to other dreamboats in future conversations about the topic at hand. Either way, once you train your ears to pick up each and every frequency coming outta the mouths of others: Buy some condoms, because people not only LURVE talking about themselves, but also boning the people who allow for and adore that.

Figure out not only what you like and believe, but the specifics of why you like/believe it—and allow that others might not agree. Take stock of yourself and your tastes, but don't consider your viewpoints immovably "correct." This makes you a person who allows for imperfection, aka a good conversationalist and also not a pigheaded, essentialist nimrod. The minute you decide that you're impermeably right about everything is the minute you shut yourself off to other kinds of interpersonal osmosis, which limits the social world around you and closes you off to all kinds of possibility and understanding. Plus, you stop learning, so you commit double homicide by also deciding it's a wrap for the development of your brain. You don't have to and probably won't buck your opinion the second you're presented with a variant one. Rather, you might become more certain of your prior conviction, and see how you communicate it in a new context, which exemplifies respect for what you believe. If you think something worthwhile and true, you are probably inclined to spread that idea, right?

Some years back, it became clearer than ever that I didn't need to mutually agree about every last one—or even most—of my beliefs, opinions, or tastes with a person in order to connect our two brains and bodies. This was thanks to a great extended sexual friendship with a Republican audio engineer named Rex. He took my boots off for me each time we got undressed, and when I was like, "Huh, dude?" he scoffed and said, "What, guys don't take your shoes offa you? You're too good for those idiots." (?!??!!! This is not a thing...as far as I know?) Rex sent my mom flowers after casually spending time with her once and taught me about Ray Charles. If I had written him off because I thought he wasn't "on the same page as me" in terms of politics, et cetera, I would have missed out on a lot, including the time we were fucking and he craned his gorgeous, craggy nose down right into my face, observing it like he was seeing me for the first time. (*Told* you it's really appreciated when you make eye contact!) After, he said that that was the distance, or lack thereof, at which I was most beautiful to him. REX! Rex ruled. Keep your mind flung wide open.

Treat people like they're smart enough to understand you by being smart enough to take in, and allow for, their difference.

You don't have to be so healthy that you ooze green-Gaia-vegetable-smoothie juice if you get a paper cut, but you have to care about your bodily well-being at least somewhat. Everyone has their own metric for what makes them feel physically and mentally sound, whether or not it includes the regular ingestion of pulverized salad-liquid. Those considerations are even less universally prescriptive if a person has a long-standing or chronic medical condition—these can include physical diagnoses like fibromyalgia, or mental ones like depression. Whatever you need to do to make yourself feel stable, and maybe even strong: Your first and most pressing responsibility in life, and sex, is to make sure you're doing those things.

I have to pester myself to drink enough water; try not to smoke; take supplements, even though the jury's out as to whether they do anything besides make me feel falsely virtuous about my commitment to *glowing, palpable immortality*; chomp my ADHD and anxiety medications because, otherwise, my brain coughs bacterially all over my happiness; get enough protein and maybe lay off the SUGARSUGARSUGAR I mainline if left to my own breakfast devices (today's morning aliments were a chocolate-chip cookie and a buttercream cupcake—I need a fucking warden). Outside of your regular routine, undertake to get yourself access to mental and/or medical help if and when you need it—in both instances, there are more options than ever out there for low-income and uninsured people now, even if they take a little research.

Illness is an insistent and recurring piece of life, no matter how fastidiously we wash the grime from our paws, take our brain-leveling psych-vitamins, or all the other millions of practices by which we try to stave off sickness. That is okay, and none of it discounts us from putting it to a healthy body when we ourselves have one again! But you have to administer to yourself, as you would any other ailing person you love, in order for that to be true. When I choose to neglect my health, others are likely to pick up on that, too. A mess, itself, is not unattractive. But a willful lack of self-regard—the nonverbal demonstration that panto-mimes the thought *I don't deserve health*—is palpable and trou-bling. How can a person confidently expect me to provide them physical kindness if I'm unwilling to do that for myself?

Don't beat yourself up if you slip, because that does nothing but make you feel even worse than the condition that cookie-cupcake breakfast combo is tormenting me with at current. If you compound sickness or discomfort with self-loathing, *that's* when you're sunk, and shame doesn't even come with the consolation of tasting amazing, rendering it entirely useless. Plus, it's under-standable: Cigarettes and candy and being so drunk that you're pretending to give a presidential address in character as Ronald McDonald are all the absolute best; you were up against Goliath here! Make a different choice next time, and keep shredding along your merry path.

Go places you love, or suspect you could love, by yourself when-ever possible. This practice guarantees, if not all new avenues of romantic or sexual possibility right then and there, that you pos-sess the three lodestars of being an attractive personage: You are intrigued by the world, motivated to pause and examine the parts of it on which your surprise and fascination snag, and you don't need anyone else to cosign your tastes in order for you to adore them. Overfeeding your day planner with the interests you find most fulfilling means you are also courting a ratcheted-up likelihood of encountering people with whom conversations will "warm up" (I know, I sound like a horny women's magazine—just go with it) quicker than the microwaved repast you'd be preparing at home if you chose ease and familiarity over discovering new shit. Not that there's anything wrong with eating out of a plastic tray. It's one of my own dearest pastimes! Albeit one that doesn't quite work for this purpose (nor, for that matter, the health tip just preceding it).

Make friends of all stripes. I used to have this problem where I held people to the loftiest of heaven-high standards for friendship. I wanted my friends to be kind, sexy party angels with spooky genius craniums, all the time, in every area of life. For the most part, I still do, and they are! But that's because I figured out the major caveat that allows the successful execution of that wish in reality: Mentally allow people to embody one or more of the above qualifiers, but not necessarily all of them, and observe the characteristics by which they emit light into the world before you do the omissions of the other ones you like in a cohort.

Expecting perfection of EVERY LAST PAL, ALL OF THE TIME, TO THE END OF MEETING EACH OF YOUR SOCIAL NEEDS AND HOPES will find you alone as heck, plus sourer than you have to be. I got tired of being unfairly let down that people were people. Trust me: Do you know how many more barbecues I got to go to once I stopped treating friendship like a military drill where, if a compatriot made one misstep, they had flunked the non-exam of "having a relationship with me"? Also, do you know how much better I feel as a person, and not just because I get to eat far more grilled meats? To demand perfection is to play yourself.

Flirt with everyone (and everything). I don't mean "flirt" as in "sleazily try to bed"—that would be extremely troublesome in this context. Flirting, to me, can mean noticing and communicating the shimmering qualities of each of life's entities. I believe the ways in which they add to the net luminosity of your day are worth big-upping.

Halfway fall in love with all the people you meet. Pick up on their most special aspects, and, when you're swooning over a person, this goes double for the parts of them that rule—of which they might not be aware others have picked up on, and would love to hear a few bromides about! Tell your colleague you love their complex acrylic nails. Say, "You look so nice today," to a mailperson who has obviously made extra time in their morning routine to embellish their uniform. Grin with just one side of your mouth at a DMV clerk who takes pains to be efficient and polite. Take a second to appreciate and mentally offer up, *God bless you, miss,* to the sun hitting the side of the bank as you walk down the street.

This swoonfest ensures that if you're sexually interested in a person you're appreciating, you'll feel so much more natural when remarking upon what it is you like about them, since you are quite used to drawing on that practice with regularity. It also ensures that you will be far happier, far more frequently—or at least whenever you stroll past the bank.

Accept invitations. This is applicable to events you have a hunch will be captivating, AND the ones that seem limp, dull, and/or grating. *Oh, you don't really like that band, so there's no probable way a person who might not agree with you about the specifics of how sound arrangements appeal to the two of you, but who is a kind and fastidious lay, might be in attendance as well?* The two have nothing to do with each other!

Going everywhere means meeting everyone, which is homiletic and useful even if you don't bone any of your fellow cult-costume party/professional conference/sociopolitical lecture/after-hours rave attendees. (All of those are places at which I've unwittingly scored.)

Become Small Deluxe

This sounds like glossolalia, or else a fast-food menu combo option, but please allow me to explain. You know how Beyoncé summoned Sasha Fierce, her more confident alternate self, in order to propel her stageward for a while? If not: For a few years, Bey created and named a personality whom she embodied during shows, then dropped off at the proscenium when she was done performing. (This is just one of many brain-ordering modi operandi that we, as a people, have appropriated from Beyoncé, who, in turn, has often copped many of them from drag queens. In terms of performing any sort of charisma, uniqueness, nerve, and talent that I might possess, I owe RuPaul just about everything I know—hell, instead of buying this book, just go send a RuQuet of roses his way on my behalf.)

This flashy self-reinvention is also a useful internal stratagem, if one that I would draw the stage curtain at actually, in our cases, discussing with other people. My perfected self-projection is called SMALL DELUXE, and I have never so much as whispered her existence into someone else's brain before today!!! AHHH! Talking about your Small Deluxe kind of undermines her purpose in that it's an admission that you have enough of a dearth of confidence to need her, but I'm willing to bring her to this party if it means we-the-world get to meet your alter ego, too. Besides, I am sustained by the knowledge that feeling perpetual and mineral certainty in oneself is a myth. If there was ever a world in which Beyoncé lacked them, you know I'm correct about this one.

I came up with Small D. one grim afternoon when I realized with horror that I had *chosen to give a psychic money* to fling some platitudes at my insecure face. I know many people find value and support in astrology, but I am not one of them—I have always hoped to be the autonomous celestial director of my own happiness, but, that day, had instead chosen to be preyed upon by a charlatan who professionally flips others' pain into cash. I examined what I had endeavored to find in the psychic's office, and the sought-after result was my best and most capable self. So I thought about what she would be like, if I could choose her (which, of course, I could and can). I envisioned how she'd respond to the circumstances I found vexing with confidence and verve, and vowed to follow her lead whenever I was feeling dented-up or otherwise low.

Small Deluxe drives a station wagon. She knows the joke doesn't have to be on anyone. She's lean and mean, but only in terms of affect, because she isn't thin. I think she has red adult braces? Not because she dislikes her teeth, but because she thinks orthodontia is beautiful, especially when it announces itself, and why not reinvent her mouth?

Who is your fake/truest person? NO, DUDE, DON'T ACTU-ALLY TELL ME. Remember, your Small Deluxe is probably most effective when kept secret.

Throw parties, even if they're not "parties." Parties exist so that the attending free agents can intermingle and leave with one another's fingerprints on their phones. Being responsible for your own bash means you have a prefab introduction to any suave-looking newcomers your guests might have rolled up with: "Hi, I'm Amy Rose! Nice to meet you—I'm glad you could make it. Where are you coming from?" WHOA NELLY with this stunningly original bon mot, I know, but its recipient is then obliged to tell you that they're happy to be there, too, and probably chat you up for a minute or two about whence they bopped, since you're the host-o-max with the inquisitive most-o-max.

You don't need to have a keg-style rager, by any means, to draw your friends and their beloved as-yet-unbeknownst-to-you cabal to the festive outpost of your choosing. Nor must you square your shoulders, put on a button-up, and cackle composedly above a glass matching all the other stemware on offer—along with your insistently self-disciplined cheerfulness—at a home brunch where no one consumes more than 1.5 cocktails per head.

What makes sense to you? What enterprises do you find unsurpassable in terms of how to invest your time? Organize a function that avails those spectacular pursuits to like-minded dreamboats: Sharing your appreciation inflates it, and has the same effect on your reputation. Have a good party or four or nine, and you will have cultivated the widespread understanding that you are a person who likes enabling others to have excellent days and/or nights. Choose what and whom you're into, and honor those selections in tandem! No themed place mats/keg taps required, unless that's the way you prefer to set your table.

Under this maxim, I started a reading series in my living room a few years back. My "Welcome Home" parties feature five rotating guests presenting excerpts of their criticism, poetry, fiction, and essays in a corner of the room as the rest of the congregation watches from my couches and floor. Then all of these like-minded superstars stay for the antecedent house parties and make out with one another, and me, in my bedroom!!! It rules. Figure out your own version of Welcome Home, get to writing out your invitations, and then, if you're hosting at your house or apartment (and that's totally optional!), clear off the stuff all over your bed in preparation—coats can find another surface to carpet.

Involve yourself in your direct community. Sex is about contact, camaraderie, and mutual esteem as much as it is getting WET 'N' WILD in the style of a smuttily named lipstick. (Confidential to makeup companies who might want to hire me someday: I sincerely adore that there are people out there whose professions are looking at a shade of unctuous pink grease and deciding, "Let's definitely call this one 'REVERSE...WOW, GIRL!'") Part of feeling communion with the world is exercised in its social microcosms. Some ways to enact this for yourself: Vote in local elections. Make friends with your deli person, corner bartender, colleagues, and neighbors.

I loathed my first office job and most of my fellow employees when I worked for a corp-o listicle website, but I took pains to identify the moments and people within it to which I could affix my limitless affections, and I left that Hades-corporation with a solid body of accomplishments in my name AND lifelong friends. In all pursuits, no matter how staid, humdrum, or even corp-o: Expand yourself by looking directly around you, and then making yourself a beautiful part of that drab-ass landscape.

Unglue your hands and eyes from your phone. When you arrive at whatever enticing place has beckoned you from out of the house, your cell phone is not your date. Put it away and pay attention for the entirety of the time you're out, save for commutes, necessary communiqués, and entering previously uncollected contact information into it. If you have to wait in a line, bring a book. If you're taking in a lecture, performance, or other event where you'd like to record notes, bring a small journal or notepad instead of pecking into your phone screen, unless a work-related reason demands otherwise. You will be more aware of, and look and feel more composed, wherever you are; being a hunched-over social-media-scroller detracts from your experience and the ability of others to differentiate you from three-quarters of the room you're in. It's less compelling, anyway. Pick up your lovely face and look the heck around!!!

Be excellent at a job—preferably one that you adore, but any position will do. Even if you're assembling drivel about being a nineteen hundred and nineties kid-lennial for a third-rate website (see: my listicle-based plight just above), do it with gusto. Self-sufficiency is the sexiest thing. If there are certain pragmatic/situational demands or restraints that keep a person from this, don't castigate yourself—given the current economic state we're collectively floundering in, I would be an utter knob-job if I didn't recognize that, in many cases, obtaining any kind of paid work, let alone in a field you love that ALSO keeps you in Diet Cokes, is pretty lucky.

Knuckle on what rent-making labor you've got, and dedicate yourself as best you can to excelling at it rather than stewing over how much you despise it. Those energies are better utilized by trying to transcend the level you're at. And don't balk at taking work that "isn't what you want to do"—I know plenty of unemployed associates whom I'm always hearing say that they're broke, but they don't want to take a part-time or entry-level position because it doesn't precisely fit the model of what career they'd like in the long run...except, when pressed as to what that is, they usually say something amorphous like, "Something creative?"

NO TO THIS. Find something—anything—that earns you the scrilla you need to scrape by, even if it's just a life-sustaining amount and no more, while you work out the specifics of that nebulous creativity or whatever it is. You'll be padding your skills, both professional and social, in the meanwhile, without depleting the mental faculties you need to do your real CREATIVE (or whatever enterprising area of inquiry you favor) work.

My greatest jobs, before I landed a dreamy one as a writer/ editor for a publication I love, have been the ones that had nil to do with my intended area of employment: Being a telemarketing-center stooge, EDM rave hostess, pizza-pushing cashier, coat salesgirl, hookah bar waitress, library page, garden-supply-store plant-hoser, events planner, et cetera, edified me as comprehensively as CREATIVE meandering-around ever has. Each position expedited my already-gnawing motivation to do something *else*, necessitated that I interact with people I wouldn't have chosen to hang with independently, and kept me (mostly) out of hock while I was at it. And they gave me things to write about, when it came time to write! Take work. Whatever you can wrangle. Not to sound TOO grandfatherly, but: It builds character. *[wheezes and asks you whatever happened to "good" music like the ol' Beatle Boys]*

Masturbate. Onanism (the sophist's preferred term for whackin' it) ensures that when you do get laid, you'll know how you like to be touched and so can more readily communicate those tastes. Masturbation is not just a means to that end, but a sheer pleasure in and of itself! (As if you didn't know this already, ya perv-ass!) It diminishes stress by releasing endorphins, aka relaxation-inducing brain chemicals, in your mind-piece (this can also help with insomnia), alleviates sexual frustration and physical tension, and is otherwise good for your health: Recent scientific studies by the University of Sydney have suggested that regular masturbation can reduce the risks of conditions like cystitis, some forms of cancer, diabetes, and certain sexual infections.* But you don't have to justify self-conducted handjobs by rationalizing that it's all for the sake of your precious medical wellness! (Although, as we have discussed: Your health is mad important.) Masturbating helps sex with people other than yourself feel like less of a looming physical obligation that isn't being met, since you're self-sufficient, pleasure-wise. Also, it feels mad good. (Again: As you know, pervadocious!!!)

Get all altruistic. You know how people sometimes sniff that volunteering and other forms of do-gooderism are *ultimately, like, so selfish in the end—they're all about making the person doing it feel good about themselves.* To this, I say: *Correct, probably! And that is so rad.* People who apply their time and energy, if they are fortunate enough to find themselves with extra supplies of these resources, to making the world the slightest bit less harrowing for others, have the right to feel good about themselves (so long as they don't post TOO many pictures of it on the internet—I don't care if people talk about the causes they love, but I rankle when that's to the end of broadcasting their own saintly virtue and generosity). Also: Who cares! Good is being done here. If, in chasing momentarily rewarding-feeling self-aggrandizement rights, a person is chipping at the net grossness of the planet's collective miseries, at least they're trying to both preen *and* big-up themselves (even if that's just internally) through fellowship. I vastly prefer this kind of grandstanding to the types of which the by-products do not serve anyone but their enactors. Like, attempting to have

---

* Staff reporter, "'Masturbation Is Good for Your Health': Experts Say It Can Prevent Conditions Such as Cystitis, Diabetes, and Cancer," Daily Mail.com, December 5, 2013, http://www.dailymail.co.uk/health/article -2518802/Masturbation-good-health-prevents-cystitis-diabetes-cancer.html.

THE HOTTEST SEX-HAIRSTYLE TO PROVE YOU'RE THE TOP DOG doesn't end up affecting anybody besides the updo-er in question, but fixing to have THE BIGGEST SEX-HEART BY DOING GOOD TURNS at least helps others out.

A secret: I used to be one of the eye-rollers who mentally (and sometimes vocally) accused people who donated time, cash, and/ or public support of being self-deifying phonies. But you know how people who are obsessed with whether the motives of others are "fake" or not are so often anxious in that way because they're fearful that expressing their own interest in similar activities is valid? When I waffled about the worth of my own motives, which were *fine*—and would have been even if they *were* narcissistic— I was stating an argument to counter what I actually believed because I was worried that if I got involved in causes I cared about, people would roll their eyes at ME. That is major dunce behavior, and it shouldn't have stopped me from just saying FUCK IT and heading down to the food pantry to see what I could do.

You don't have to "volunteer" quite so overtly, either. As I mentioned, not everyone has that temporal luxury—and maybe you don't WANT to plant a rain forest on an oil spill! Find your own version of answering to the itchy beliefs you're inclined to scratch at most persistently by quizzing yourself thusly: *Did I add worth and/or goodness to another person's life today?* If the answer is yes: You are closer to whole than you would have been otherwise, and more appealing, because there is nothing hotter than a person unafraid of actively executing what they think is true.

Treat life's quotidian-seeming offerings and tasks like parties, or at least non-annoyances. This concept is similar to macking on every single piece of your encountered universe. If you dress for errands, greet your commute with a rapacious sense of...if not avidity, at least tolerant acceptance (and hand sanitizer), and clean your room with as close to zeal as you can muster, you triangulate your proficiency in meeting real-McCoy celebrations and social gatherings with ease and grace. Plus, take it from the don himself, the writer David Foster Wallace, whose "This Is Water" speech-turned-book included this bulletproof aphorism: "If you've really learned how to think [...] it will actually be within your power to experience a crowded, hot, loud, slow, consumer-hell-type situation as not only meaningful, but sacred, on fire with the same force that lit the stars—compassion, love, the subsurface unity of all things." Imagine meeting a person who comported themselves this way—what could prove their sexiness more convincingly than the assured belief that everything is divine, even if it blows tuna chunks? I have a wonderful bulletin for you: You don't have to *meet* that person to experience the gratification that comes with translating "consumer hell" into "star-arson" when you can just choose to *be* that person instead. Also, complaining is off-putting unless you're already in love, in which case you've both made a compact that you get to bitch to each other; opt for perceiving annoyances as meaningful/sacred instead whenever you can.

At the risk of sounding like a warm slice of cornbread, I present the final and most crucial of all these sexiness-inducing life rules: LIFE RULES. You don't have to convey that by trying to morph into some sunny, uncritical goon who is NEVER in a bad mood, 100 percent into their surroundings, or best friends with each and every conscious being they encounter. But you can use whatever pieces of the above strategies to identify, chase after, and highlight the parts of yourself and your life to which you grant the most merit. Prioritize them, and you're bound to cross bods with plenty of salacious compatriots who find them worth responding to in sexual overtures, too.

From the Inside Out

When you launch yourself into the world you've chosen, there's no need to do so with the first-priority end goal of getting it in with a fellow world-attendee. But there are certainly times when you'll turn around to find: *There is someone beautiful here.* What will you say to them? Because, look, you *are* going to go up to them. If that seems intimidating: Rejection is the universe's protection, as a creaky adage goes. Whether or not you're aggravated by platitudes, this one is accurate—you can court dismissal as doggedly as you do success, because it's just as good for you… and a little easier to accomplish, hee! If you sidle up to someone with a genteel, well-intentioned manner about you, then it's their decision as to whether their personality meshes with the truth of what you're presenting. If it doesn't, that's fine, and the only thing you've "lost" is the non-opportunity to have sex with someone who doesn't get you.

On Winking

I find friendly winking totally harmless and equal parts coy and magnetic, and so do the solid handful of people I've picked up after *I closed my eye at them suggestively.* (When you break down the facts of this pick-up move: How is it sexy?! I love the world sometimes.) Winking is ridiculous, but at least it's not meek.

We're livin' in a weird zone, more so than ever, when it comes to gauging whether someone wants to hook up or just hang out. Luckily, everyone is trying to squint through the same murky atmosphere to ascertain this. It can be a relief to have someone just tell you what they want. Being amorously point-of-fact reads as daring—even courageous. It distinguishes you as a deliberate and self-assured character, aka the sexiest kind of person.

The main tenet of nonchalantly scamming on cool babes is acting like you know and agree that you are a person others would be stoked to be close to, even if you don't, in fact, know/agree with that. Per Kurt Vonnegut, "We are what we pretend to be," and that extends to acting like your face is 10 times hotter than you think it is while maintaining your specific personal charms. Eight times out of ten, if you introduce yourself to a new person, assume some air of great purpose about you, and tell them something honest and enticing in its irregularity (especially if it also happens to be funny), that person will talk to you. If they're receptive to your flirtatious attempts at conversation, then probably two times out of that eight, minimum, you can kiss them if you want later on. (These are bullshit statistics culled from the field. I am not a numbers guy, but they feel really true?)

You can safely presage action so long as you ask enough questions to allow another person to be up front, which is to say, bizarre—and laugh at their jokes, especially if they're bad as much as they are sweet. Two of my favorite lines that amorous strangers have chanced my way: "If you were a hamburger at McDonald's, I would call you McBeautiful"; "I want to make out with you in a kitchen made of fur." McBeautiful here entertained both prospects, even if the re-fur-idgerator was only theoretical—I just started picturing it, and next thing you know, I was sucking face. It was trancelike; disorienting. If either had chosen to blandly say, instead, "Hello, you're hot and also sexy, and I like that about you," I would have been less amenable to their advances, plus creeped out about their odd, forward, and formal choices of language.

Being forthcoming has its merits if you do it right. You have to jazz an introductory statement up a little, but I still believe in making your intentions more or less clear. Liking that someone is *hot and also sexy* is not enough, seduction-wise, as its own sentiment. Bluntness takes some maneuvering, and when you've made a pointed effort toward cleverness, it carries the subtext of respect. It demonstrates that you're allowing room for conversational parrying, which is so often the gateway to *ssseduction*.

When I'm introducing myself to a vulpine stranger, I look them squarely in the face with an expression on my own that says, "DAAANG WITH ALL THAT, YA FOX." After our initial name-exchange and other hey-how-are-yas, if it's just the two of us talking and not a big group in front of which this person might feel embarrassed or put on the spot, I let my intended know what I find captivating about them. This can be as general—"I like your hair"—or as specific as you see fit. Be sure to drop your compliment(s) casually and then keep the conversation moving, as though you just emitted some drab remark about the doggone weather, and can now get to the heart of a conversation, having put the necessary small talk behind you. Give them time to say "thank you," or let them protest, but then say, "Ha! So...," and then advance with the encounter, having nicely established your motivations here while also having given them room to play along.

Making good conversation hinges on actually having something to say. If you're digging around in your brain-pockets for some loose change plus a fossilized piece of gum–type thoughts to offer up, *stop*. Do not do what I often do and unspool at the mouth like a pair of windup chattering teeth! "The fact that it's raining outside today is kind of like this city's baseball team that I know nothing about in actuality, huh? Heh...h-heh," is a verbal mess providing no hint as to what's intriguing about you. Instead, be intrigued by *them*. Taking a vested interest in the hot person at hand won't be hard, since it's already *truthfully how you feel*. You're all about getting to know them, so ask questions like you're a paradoxically laconic and laid-back investigative reporter. ("Oh, the big scoop? Yeah, I got it...just a minute.")

The easiest question in the world: "How was your day?" Even if it's matched with the easiest answer in the world, the dreaded and static-at-best, untrue-at-worst "good," you can volley it back without seeming like a voyeur or a try-hard: "Oh, yeah? What'd you do?" If they say, "Oh, I worked/went to school/hung out with some friends," don't wilt yet. They're still talking to you! They're likely just shy, so don't take their cue and cover up the nuance of their personality, like, *Ugh, this person is a dullard who is indentured to a thudding, plain-gelatin-flavored life and mind.* That's harsh, plus false, since no one really is.

I recently met a person from out of town with whom I have a mutual friend, and though I didn't want to bone him, I make a habit of enjoying this miniature-personal-history-style introduction regardless of from whom I'm extricating it. A few days later, our mutual friend ran into the person I had spoken with, and my pal told me that the latter effused, "Amy Rose was THE BEST!" I couldn't remember having performed any particularly dazzling feat and am also an occasional ham sandwich, so I asked why he had seen fit to indirectly make my day. "He's been hanging with all his tightest old friends all week, but you're the only person who asked him how he was and concentrated on the answer." I glowed to my furthest corners at hearing this...and wasn't too sad for that guy, because I'm sure none of his long-standing friends meant to slight him, plus, he *did* get asked by somebody in the end! It was cheering to have been that person.

There are all kinds of variants on this informal model for demonstrating sincere curiosity about a person, too. I'm reluctant to link attraction and career work, because that assigns sexual value to something that can be pretty mechanical and/or bureaucratic, but if you're not as precious about this, another version of the aforementioned question is, "What are you working on lately?" You can—and should—specify that you don't necessarily mean *within a profession*: I do this by leading, "Man, it's so nice to be out of the house tonight—I've been so focused on this one heroic couplet [insert your own less revolting priorities here!]." Then fire off the above question, having left room that can be filled by your interest's non-vocational pursuits. Also useful: "How do you know the host?" "Are you familiar with this band/artist/whatever?" "How did you get involved with [whatever you're both doing]?" As long as your prompt cannot be successfully met with the word "yes" or "no," you're doing a valiant job at this.

Kid around about a person's answers whenever you can—being funny or at least playful works muscularly in the favor of getting you laid—but most important is taking in what a person is saying to you in response instead of inwardly composing the witticisms you're about to lob back. What is even the point of talking to others if you're just concerned about what comes out of you next? Conversation should be allowed to race along directionlessly, and that's unlikely to happen if anybody's overthinking it. Stick to general questions with personalized answers, then ditch the script. Act under the thought that you *do* want to hear what the person has to say, without expectation. And mean it, as much for your sake as for theirs! They might, after all, say something that changes your mind about their boneability. But let's continue as though this is a negligible potential outcome. (If it is: Treat yourself with the same regard, affection, and attention you would someone else, and respect your feelings—just because you established this flirtation-station doesn't mean you have to see it through.)

After you charm in your singular, polite way, disappear for a moment. Dip to the bar, bathroom, or another conversation to allow your intentioned brain/body-latcher the pleasure of seeking you. You know how when you have a crush, it's your captor? When you like or want to get with somebody, you feel this churning happy bereft desperation: THAT PERSON EXISTS, AND I NEED THEM NEAR ME SO I CAN AFFIX MYSELF TO THEM EITHER PHYSICALLY OR BY LATCHING BRAINS. That feeling is what life is for. At its core, it's *ambition*, which is borne of a *lack* of something—or someone. Let the other person cultivate the insistent *lack* of your knowing each other, whether the capacity in which that'll be is to be "casual" (read: orgasm-related) or more sustained, in tandem with you.

Okay! Let's say all's swell, you've hung out and established a mutual attraction, and are now hoping to abscond to the bone zone (wherever that may be for you—your place, theirs, the back-seat of someone's Buick, etc.). When you feel the time is right, phrase your proposal by framing it as an offer of a different breed—saying "Let's go home and fuck" *can* work (and has for me before), but much like tempering your initial approach with a bit of discretion, you'd do better to posit the idea that you should share a trip to your next immediate locale (read: BONE-A-ZONA) for a more innocuous purpose. None of these propositions, if accepted, guarantee sex (because not-nothin' does that besides verbalized consent), but the honey in question is likely intelligent enough to pick up the subtext of what these suggestions mean. Depending on what you've been up to, say, "Do you want to go listen to records/have a glass of wine/make some coffee/smoke a joint at [X SEX LOCALE]?" See what unfolds from there.

The above proviso works beautifully for one-night stands, which can easily turn into longer courtships/extended engagements if you're both so inclined. However, though I do not buy the idea that someone forsakes the prospect that you are a person of value that incites prolonged interest if you deign to submit thine precious flesh upon first meeting them, I like to attenuate the mystery if I want to see somebody again. I don't recommend dishonesty, but it's worth noting that the majority of the romantic relationships I've ever had, successful or otherwise, have come from waiting for at least one more rendezvous before getting more physical than making out. Instead of inviting a new person straight over, I'll agree to share a cab, but depart alone at my destination instead of continuing a dual ride home or asking them up. I'll flirt back a bit less aggressively or otherwise insert some distance when a person thinks for sure that they've got me in the bag (and when I'm like, "BUT THEY DO—AM I KID-DING MYSELF? THEY ARE A BASTION OF PERFECTION," I remember that anyone can literally bone any flirtation-mate they want—"leagues" don't exist as long as you behave like they don't).

If I do like them a lot straight out of the gate, I might say, "Sure, we can go out. I think I'm free in eight days?" I have meant this every single last solitary time I've said it. That's because I have a life to lead—meeting a cute person doesn't have to crown them the monarch of your head. You still have friends to see later that night/some sleep to catch (the taxi goodbye)/a business trip to California to make (Hanukkah-length SEE YA LATER)/or other people to break it off with in order to respect their feelings (the guy who texted me, "Wow your super anti huh," which no one says unless they are profoundly about it, while I took my time kindly ending things with another person—which I was doing anyway, I solemnly swear). If you would like to stretch this to longer than a night without having to employ these pretenses and have shared a significant deal of interesting and intriguing time together already, just fail to say goodbye when you leave. Nothing incubates a fledgling crush like ghosting out on it.

If they *don't* sleuth you down by the next evening, follow or friend them on social media, or otherwise bat-signal, "Hiiiiiiii thar." If another day passes, write a brief note: "You have a funny way of saying goodbye." This is the only subterfuge I am will-ing to recommend, and only because it works so well. On the off chance they don't write back, leave it—rejection is the condom of the universe &c. If they do, WE'VE GOT A LIVE ONE HERE. What you do now is all on you, McBeautiful.

Introducing Everyone

Online dating can be a laborious hell-venture. It can also get you VERY laid if you simply prod at your cell phone a few times. The latter might sound like an appealing premise, but it's also one of the reasons that I don't recommend it unless you live somewhere remote, are queer (homos tend to be more capable at acting like actual humans on the cold, vast internet—we often need to, because of scarcity and safety, even in big cities)—or are a thick-skinned pillar of resilience who doesn't mind being told to "show me ur ass cheexz."

That's right, me friend: I'm one of those knuckle-dragging curmudgeons who believe that, whenever possible, in-person tom-catting is where it's at. As with every way of relegating tasks that used to be done in person to the solitary convenience of your com-putron, the online method is desocializing—unless it's your *only possible means* of socializing. In order to curtail my online spending habits, for example, I stuck a note to my computer that reads "REMEMBER THAT EVERY TIME YOU BUY SOMETHING OFF OF THE INTERNET, YOU ARE ROBBING YOURSELF OF A STRANGER." Unless I cannot find the sought-after item in person, this tiny imperative reminds me that whatever low cost Amazon is luring me in with is actually unaffordable, because it keeps the world and me apart.

Many of my friends have culled a love that is truly bulletproof from among the gnashing gyre of the dating internet, but if you're just looking to get nailed and nail in kind, then I think you should hit the streets. "LOOK HERE, YOU LUDDITE," you could pro-test, "I am painfully socially inept! I could never screw up the nerve to drop myself in front of a babe in the flesh!" I see and feel and know and, so often of the time, *are* you, my dude. That's why I can tell you that it's crucial—essential—that you don't widen that shyness via the curt binary of ACCEPTANCE/REJECTION that online dating cultivates. Do you think it's going to do wonders for your taciturn, self-winnowing introversion to bob around in a system that turns people into baseball cards? To send out a well-curated sample of yourself, and then plotz when even that miniature clipping of you withers under the rejections of people whose misspellings are so difficult to decipher that you can barely tell which vulgarity they're attempting to lob at you? (This inevitably happens to everyone and is not a commentary on you; it's a part of all boning endeavors, but especially this one.)

If you are inhibited by tendencies toward convenience, or meekness, catering to that won't help you change it. Shut down your computer and thrust yourself into the outside world, which has not only most of the same people you'd have encountered online striding around in it, but also plenty of others. While you can absolutely have hot sex ordered on-screen with the help of your internet provider, part of what makes being your own sexual pioneer so revelatory is the discovery that there are all varieties of smokin'-hot and willing voyagers looking to cross your physical path.

The bright side of online dating is that it makes those who are friendly and cool as they hit on people in the flesh seem brave and self-possessed for well-executed macking. This is not to say that online dating is *ab*normal. It's rightfully accepted as the territory of sane, well-adjusted, and pleasant people, where once it held the stigma of the exclusive homeland of the interpersonally maladapted, which was as unfair (and mean, and reductive) back in the internet's infancy as it is now. I hope it doesn't feel like I'm contributing to that stigma! I do feel that the internet can be a wonderful conduit for getting in touch with like-minded horny people (who are not me). But if you have the means to meet those selfsame kinds of crush-inducers in person, I find it to be so much sexier when you're able to get a feel for what their voices sound like, how they move across a room (especially from the back, heyyy), the purposeful gestures they conduct with their hands, the graceful shapes their mouths form as they talk . . . because I, as you can probably tell after that in-depth little daydream, am the perviest of them all!!!

So you're putting your shoes on and ready to head out the door to . . . *Wait, where do sexually viable people even congregate?* Your first guess is correct: If you're not feeling creative when it comes to striking out into the world, I have met many paramours in bars. So many bars, a cavalcade of bars, a city-populating-if-you-amassed-their-clientele amount of bars bars *bars* bars bars. If you're sober and avoiding those places, disinterested in hanging out lounge lizard–style, or just bored of the bar barrage: I am happy to report that THE WHOLE REST OF THE WORLD EXISTS.

Context matters here. You can meet somebody anyplace, hence my advocating that you create your own palatial life to hang out inside. Just in case you need initial ideas on this tip, though, here's a selection of unlikely-seeming places where I have scammed on, or been scammed on, to good success:

• **Bookstores.** If you see a babe milling around, ask them for recommendations. Done and done. I have met two paramours between bookshelves—and was also introduced to Dylan Thomas's short fiction by one of my book-marks, the greatest outcome of them all. I thought that dude only wrote poetry! And I got laid!

• **The ever-lovin' sidewalk.** I had the best sex of my life, easily, resplendently, world- and game-changingly, with a person whom I met loitering curbside.

I was at an after-party for an out-of-town work conference, and everyone was standing outside on the sidewalk because watching a group of writers dancing can begin to seem cruel after the first few minutes (keep in mind that mine is a breed of people who spend most of their time alone indoors). This should also persuade you that if I, a native to this taciturn, housebound clan, can get laid by a coincidental chance meeting, it should be cake for everybody else.

On this particular evening, two editors walked up to my friends and me. One of these men I had not previously met. I interjected my hand and misunderstood the introduction proffered as he shook it: "Brafe? It's 'Brafe'?" *I actually asked this*, even though in no conceivable dialect or tongue is that an intelligible name for a human male, furthering the point that my getting laid can serve as a font of hope for the rest of the general population, and that maybe if, as a writer by career, I also lack the basic facilities of speech, maybe the dancing thing is more of a "me" problem than a professional one.

The human male in question corrected me graciously: He was really called *Jake*, but we agreed that he'd keep my updated appellation, and that he, in turn, would call me "Emro," close in pronunciation to "Elmo." I noticed he was fiddling with his hair, which fell to his shoulders, and also that he had an abdomen reminiscent of an Italian sculpture. He watched me take stock of both and asked me for a ponytail holder, which he sent me a picture of after sleuthing out my contact information the next day. (I never give out my contact when I know someone can find it—it's part of the fun, and they almost always make good on it.) As far as Brafe and I were concerned: *It was absolutely on.*

Or, it would be. We met up later at a different party, and he rented a luxury sports car so we could drive through some nearby snowcapped mountains (?!??!?!!!), but I had an unforeseen conflict come up preventing the joyride. (I have cursed not having just canceled those less-fun plans for the rest of eternity.)

All was not lost. A week or so later, when we had both returned to our home city, I agreed to meet him at his apartment. It was a mansion of a unit. The building had the name TRUMP emblazoned on its edifice, and it was dim and choked with paintings and pianos inside. Brafe emerged into the doorjamb, and he looked even better than I remembered—and my mental configuration of his features and body was already in its fullest overactive thrall. We didn't even have time to say hello.

(Brafe, if you're reading this: Thanks for the follow-up texts, dude, but I didn't want to see you again because it was so gargantuanly perfect that one time that I didn't want to risk altering the memory, which . . . I'm now infuriated by how ferociously boneheaded that decision was. I still can't believe you post-coitally played me Backstreet Boys on the piano while singing along in perfect pitch. The sex was also that perfect, times about 72.) (Brafe, were you even real?) (Call me, Brafe.)

• **The fried chicken spot near my house.** At Palace Fried, the guys behind the counter call me "Miss Spicy" and can recite my phone number from memory, but not because I use this place as a pick-up spot. It's because I order a spicy chicken sandwich three to four times a week when my vegetarianism is lapsing particularly exceptionally . . . wait, wait. No. It's *definitely* because of this. Goddamnit.

Any solid nickname is borne of a reputation. I first earned this one on some summer night. I had just come from a tepid party next door and was in no great rush to return—I had dipped for chicken upon hearing a cluster of bona fide adults literally talking about their SAT scores, *shudder.* A guy was in front of me in line, and as we waited for our respective three-piece and characteristic spicy chicken, I noticed that he was wearing a Hüsker Dü shirt. Since I am, apparently, still of the seventh-grade mindset that if a person likes what you're into musically, they are definitely meant to come home and neck with you, I complimented it. We got to talking. Then we got to eating our drumsticks together, and I decided to see what would happen if I told him that my apartment was around the corner if he might like to drop by real quick. Smash cut to us smashing, then cheerily parting forever. (Dear Hüsker Dü: I love you even more now, which I did not think previously possible. Ever yours, Miss Spicy.)

• **Concerts.** If I am willing to come out and advocate for capitalizing on common musical tastes as shared at a scrappy purveyor of breaded poultry, please trust I find it even easier to do so at venues that more straightforwardly celebrate the musical acts I love. Just go up to some hot person and talk about the lineup, or related acts, or other shows you've seen at the outlet in which you're both standing. I have gotten laid via this brand of taxonomizing/cultural fetishism more times than I can now recall.

• **Tasteful midafternoon parties at an accomplished colleague's or associate's house.** For me, these situations are rare enough that I feel it's my duty to capitalize on them each and every time they go down. Here's what to do: Compliment the wristwatch/necklace of the person with the crispest-looking pocket square or pastel lipstick if you're into an older, august sexual partner. If you choose to become the conduit for a member of the bourgeoisie's "normal-person" fetish, that usually guarantees very very very scandalous sex or your white wine with one ice cube back. If getting off on condescension and class rage is not your thing, which, HIGHLY understandable: You are surrounded by a supremely hot waitstaff composed of peers from class and age brackets that, in all likelihood, are more closely concentric to your own. These heroes are bored, stoned, and used to being alternately verbally pissed on/hit on by the aforementioned upper-crusters. Given all three conditions, you will be an even more welcome refreshment than the pitchers of mint julep set jauntily on each wicker table. Depending on how flossy your venue is, there may even be additional needless help-for-hire around: I fooled around with a twenty-four-year-old event photographer with literally nothing else to do on a lawn swing at a super-tony house last summer, thanks to the misguided largesse of the overstaffed host, and it was the most memorable fete of the summer...maybe the host was cannier than I realized at the time? Was this just another way in which they provided for their guests? Crafty.

• **Non-bourgeois-friends' parties.** This interpersonal configuration is a winsome option because you've got prior intelligence as to whom the guest list might roll call. If you don't, that's lovely just the same: You already know that your friend is a mensch, so by the laws of the transitive property, they almost definitely mix with others whom you'll find beguiling, too. Save for public cement walkways, this is my preferred venue when it comes to traversing a landscape rife with french-worthy individuals. I have met scads of hookups on my one friend John's roof alone—in the summertime, he has a party every week or two on average, and you likely have some analogous person like this in your life: Go see who's around.

Here's a list of less-advisable spots where I've made introductions to, or been approached by, sensual collaborators. Forging a connection is feasible nearly anywhere on earth—with some caveats in place. Let's talk context about the following meeting spots:

• **Public transportation.** This one is a gamble, and you have to be discerning, because most of the time, people are taking the train to or from work. If you're into women, be ESPECIALLY conscious of the fact that you are one of forty-two others peering at any attractive female-bodied person in whatever your vicinity is, and it's best to be among the often slim fraction of those who are decent enough to not do or say anything to express that. If you MUST hit on a fellow passenger, passing notes is less horrible than expecting someone to talk to you, especially when your miniature letter just says "oh my god you are so gorgeous" and you look up and the person won't meet your eyes because they're blushing so much, as one memorable guy in a sexy yellow sweater proved to me. Trains are better for furtive glances back and forth across the car that you can then fantasize about for the rest of your life than they are for trying to fulfill those daydreams.

• **The company for which you work.** I've undeniably had heaps of sex with colleagues and peers outside of my direct professional biznet (what "in-the-know" corporate insiders like me call "business networks"). So please trust me when I say that getting with coworkers whom you see five days out of the week is pretty dicey—and also one of the sexiest known kinds of entanglements, so long as the two biznetters are smart enough to keep their less-than-professional connection secret, which ramps up the hotness quotient by an enormous margin and has the additional perk of ensuring that you both don't wind up unemployed.

I had two and a half work side-pieces when I worked in an office of the same size and genial temperament as the Death Star, and it made going to work far more bearable. I wouldn't recommend this at smaller companies, or if there's a significant power differential between the two employees who are hard at work. I would never have sex with a subordinate or a boss, because the prospect that there would be some subtext of expectation based on one person's higher-ranking title is too exploitative to follow through with on good faith. If this person works in an unrelated department or is on the same professional plane, though? Use your judgment—your job is (usually) more important than ones that begin with "hand" or "blow," but there have been instances where I went right ahead and hooked up in the third-floor conference room that no one uses anyway. Consider discretion an unspoken point on the "skill sets" segment of your resume, and you'll likely be fine.

• **Planet Hollywood in scenic Orlando, Florida.** Other odds were working against me, too—like, his name was Gilbert, but I remained undeterred—at least I heard it right that time.

• **The Willowbrook Mall in Wayne, New Jersey.** Please just trust me on this one, and exponentially more so when it comes to the Ruby Tuesday's on the premises, in specific. Heed my word and do not fuck at this mall.

• **If you are me: the dating internet.** Tinder is convenient if you're traveling and want to get it on with a stranger, but so, too, are the long-running industry standard for traveling dirtbags, aka—all together on this one, now—bars. If you don't meet anyone there, you can at least have a vodka and maybe some small plates (buffalo wings), and Tinder still exists, should you not feel contented making out with buttery hot sauce exclusively.

No matter the course you set, the beginning of that path is easy to follow: Go outside. Smile at someone who looks like your interpretation of the term "super-babe." If they smile back, all you have to do is refer to our trusty old prompt: "Hey. How's your day going?" Then see if you just happen to have the best sex of your life (mishearing your partner's name: optional).

No, I Still Want to Lick a Face from the Web

If you remain unconvinced of the superiority of physical encounters and you're still looking for a technological helping hand: I often ghostwrite my friends' profiles and messages back and forth with hot .jpg-havers and have been described identifiably on my city's Missed Connections page enough that you could probably make an identical composite sketch of my face from the combined information within the listings. (I responded once—enormous error on my part. I thought the dude was cute and the moment we shared on the train borderline romantic, but he texted me asking me for my best "cow jokes" [???] for nearly six months.)

I feel conflicted about abetting the probable shucking-off of kismet/coincidence/mystery by giving you the following information, but look: *I will get you laid on the computer*, Luddite or not—although the fact that I unwittingly just wrote "on the computer" like your granddad, instead of the infinitely less geriatric "the internet" or "online," should be proof enough of my technological proficiency and tastes. Whatever. Let's hit the ol' digital web for some sensual cyber-chat!!!

While the internet has its fungal pockets, so, too, does EVERY OTHER COLLECTION OF PEOPLE GROUPED IN ONE PLACE. There are many lovelinesses who are, at this moment, saying, "OK, Cupid—I guess, dude." That name has always seemed SO ambivalent, when the precipice of sex = more than just an "okay" state in which to spend time, in my estimation. This is a digression, but how the heck am I supposed to be enthusiastic if the COMPANY ITSELF is all passively like, "Eh, it'll kill twenty minutes, this whole multitudinous-possibilities-for-interpersonal-connection thing."

How can you tell if someone is decent or just *masquerading* as a preschool teacher with nice hands that they don't intend to employ for the purpose of murking you out? Honor your instincts, even if they seem overactively guarded. It's *good* that you want to protect yourself. More on this in the part of the book in which I talk about how not following that imperative once led me to an unfortunate encounter in a pool painted to look like outer space—evidence that real-life courtship can be just as fetid as poorly vetted internet dalliances.

If your cretin-meter isn't chirping at you and you're just concerned as to the *quality* of a potential internet-based lay, check for any overtly ablaze disaster flares, judgment-wise: Does their default photo find them "jokily" reenacting a meme with a disoriented-looking elderly woman (their grandmother?) near a pile of brownish dirty laundry? Are they strangely cryptic, or straightforwardly obfuscating, as to their age? Do they write *anything at all* about the preferred weight of their match-to-be? Given their lack of consideration in any of those capacities, I would also wager that you wouldn't extract much enjoyment from any sexual encounter you shared with that person.

It's pretty easy to avoid inspiring a similar snap judgment in those perusing your profile photos. As we know, the elements of just about every site or app intended to put another warm body in the space occupied by your phone are usually thus: at least one photo and a truncated description of yourself, both of which communicate that you fuck like you're tryna earn a degree for it. Here's how to achieve that:

- Include your face and the upper half of your body.
- Wear something that makes you feel like a sexual comet.
- That's pretty much it! (I find that the less background and more PERSON in the picture, the more attention-locking it is.)

Visual motifs to avoid:

• If you are genuinely interested in internet liaisons, why would you decide that a picture of your pet hanging out by itself makes a great default? It's cool if there's a fur-face IN the picture (although you might alienate those with allergies...but who wants to have that conversation re: casual sex anyway?). Reconsider offering up your pet when asked to provide documentation of your sweet face, because no one wants to have sex with your cat (I truly hope).

• Bottles of alcohol, especially in "club"-lookin' environs. It's cool—I love getting plastered, too. But making this the MAIN ELEMENT that you highlight in a photo—that you are not only of legal drinking age, but that you intend to show it off!!!—comes off like you might not have that much of a personality otherwise, or might not have the presence of mind to remember that you do.

• Pick a profile photo that is free of not only elderly family members and domesticated animals, but of other people in general, so that a person doesn't message you under the misunderstanding that you are your photo-mate; geriatric or not. Even if you think it's fairly obvioso to tell just who is whom, it's also considerate not to put your close ones' pictures online for scoring-based purposes. Crop if you have to.

• Do not post pictures where there is any kind of visible mess or clutter in the background. I get that not everybody has a design-magazine-level home (unlike me, a person whose bedroom definitely doesn't have one of those weird fake "office" ceilings, a three-layer wallpaper palimpsest, and a cat door). That's okay, as long as you keep it off the internet: Detectable untidiness in profile photos distracts from your dreamy face and tempers it with messiness. You are too good-looking for that, I think.

• Any materials that find you itching to prove that you are a Good Person™, such as the likenesses of the patients you treat in illness-stricken foreign nations. No one needs to see your self-righteousness quite that clearly, dude. Ew. I was trying to bone, not spend a half hour talking about how you "really felt like a part of *their* community" and then having to ask you to leave.

• Babies. It's great if parents want to use the internet to enjoy themselves! But to draw the link between sex and children so overtly feels like a bit much. So, too, does the judgment of a parent showcasing their child as part of their hunt for sexual escapades.

• Guns. No guns, please. I cannot believe I even have to write this. Actually, you know what? Go ahead. If you are a person of the opinion that firearms are not only a worthy but essential element to your profile picture, please go right ahead and keep the gun in the picture, so that the rest of us can stay the heck away from you, ya lunatic.

How to write and respond to messages: Everyone hates a form letter. Isn't it even *more* enraging when some creditor, insurance company, or whatever entity is mailing you what used to be a tree but is now garbage tries to make their effort look "homemade" or personalized by using a font that's supposed to resemble handwriting or pretending they know your life based on where you live? YOU'RE A *BANK*, asshole. You are not my friend, Capital One, so do not address me as such in your spamvelopes.

Getting a copied-and-pasted missive on a dating site is similarly insulting and tone-deaf, as far as I've heard. This makes good sense to me, especially if it's just some variation on "sup," the most irritating and expectant manner of "hitting on" someone in recorded history. The writers of "sup" are leeches! They are placing the onus wholly on the other person to come up with some witty retort, and those recipients don't even know that they have a reason to bother yet! Actually, they have the opposite, since "what's up" is an instant boner-killer.

Some people use a more expansive template, but when the reader can tell it's a dating Mad Lib all the same, the sender often may as well not have bothered. What you might do instead of copying the suave and flirtatious moves of institutions shilling credit cards: Comment on the aspect of a person's profile that genuinely attracted you to begin with, like a certain interest or mutual trait, compliment the person's appearance without going full-skeeve-overboard in the ass-cheexz direction, and ask them a question about something in their profile that they seem to have spent thought and time devising. Hollering at someone on the internet is easy: Keep it short, spell correctly, and don't be a bank.

If the person messages back and seems cool, your online interactions should end with one more communiqué, and that's it! The longer you go back and forth without putting voices, faces, and inflections to your conversation, the greater the opportunity to conjure false or misleading versions of yourselves. Ask them out! Propose an activity that you think they'd like based on what they've chosen to say about themselves in their profile—much like "sup," open-ended requests to hang, as in interrogating them about what they'd like to do, make them do your work for you. Conversely, asking to spend time with them decisively demonstrates that you know what you're doing, and that they'd probably like to do whatever that is with you. Suggest something specific, and then say that you're down to try out some other pursuit if what you've floated isn't of interest.

When you're the one responding to an introductory message like the ones conceptualized above, you're in a far easier position. A nice, optional guideline: Even if, like me, you're not naturally funny, come at your reply with levity and/or wryness. Thank them for writing you. Ask a question, and make it specific to them in the style laid out above. Then let them chase you! The fun of being wanted is similar to the fun of wanting. With luck, a person will come to experience both. The whole point of these endeavors is good sex, and the whole point of good sex is realizing that you can position and reposition yourself as you go.

How to Graciously Turn Someone Down

Save for the cases in which you're flagged down by catcallers and "suitors" with defunct understandings of what qualifies as a compliment, turning people down with kindness is an admirable practice. *You* might not have the kind of tender nerves that make hitting on someone feel like a potentially humiliating risk, but don't make the assumption that everyone else shares your unflappability! Even if the person wooing you is grounded and easy about any potential negative reaction, it's still less than preferable to have someone sneer into their drink at your advances. Say, "Thanks, but I'm not interested," like a self-actualized adult.

If someone invades your space, interrupts or touches you without asking, or comes at you clumsily, you do not owe them your politeness, as they haven't paid any mind to yours. In those cases, I like to crisply pronounce every letter in the phrase "You need to back up," while looking at the offending party like I want to garnish them with parsley and masticate 'em. That's usually enough to get the shitheel to slur, "SOH-RRY!" and maybe call me a bitch, then leave. Perfect!

Whom Should You Bone?

Anyone who's lucky enough that you should want to. I was going to add, "...as long as they seem like a good person," but who needs goodness when sometimes you want an encounter to carbonate what you think sexual quality is all about? Often, if you allow the opposite of what you would have engineered to happen without trying to apply the grid of "What You Like" onto it, you find that that framework has more elasticity than you thought. Like, did you know, heretofore until you pinioned your limbs around the person you're boning, that you were into being bitten like one of those shockingly oversized turkey legs at a county fair, as aggressed by a guy named Ron with something to prove? You did not. Now, you're sure of it.

Allow for the chance for every word in "What You Like" to change meanings whenever you have sex. The act of "what" you're doing, the "you" who knows only how they've gone about sex with people who aren't the person they're salivating about in the current moment, and whether "liking" something includes finding room to make it worthy of attention besides, "THIS IS WHAT HAD HAPPENED TO ME SO FAR THAT IS COMPARABLE TO NO-CLOTHES-TIMES I HAD SEEN AT THE MOVIES WHERE THE PEOPLE WERE VERY 'MTV BEACH BODY CALIFORNIA' HOT, WHICH I LIKED." Keep things mutable, and you'll maximize your happiness.

That mindset also applies to having a "type" when it comes to sexual partners. Usually, if someone I'm involved with seems to be pantomiming the choreography of porn *without* including me in their mimicry, I'm not hooking up with them again. I also don't sleep with people who perpetuate, or in any way behave like they generally agree with, bigoted slurs/acts of any category. Barring larger discussions about consent, physical aggression, and so on, these are my only mineral rules.

Other more flexible demographics to consider:

• **People who you can mostly bet are accomplished experts in bed:** under-thirty drivers of station wagons, not DJs, dudes whose nail polish matches another element of their outfits, *any* person with short, clean fingernails (varnished or not), lockpickers, piano players, anyone of *any* hand-based vocation, ballerinas, gymnasts, wearers of loafers with no socks in the summer (even if their feet smell), thoughtful upholders of spinal posture (my endless wolf-whistles, once again, to eye contact–maintainers, as well), adults with spotless orthodontia, people who prefer going to the movies instead of watching them at home, girls with Morrissey pompadours, guys with Morrissey pompadours, anyone with a Morrissey pompadour, youngs in overalls (if they're not wearing anything underneath, bring them home *as soon as you can*), people with nicknames that would also be at home on the hull of a speedboat, fixers of small household appliances, sewers of their own clothing, the guy at the supermarket who smiles with every part of his face except his mouth and you can tell it's because he's shy about his beautifully haywire teeth, listeners of the radio.

• **People around whom you should padlock your thighs closed:** most career music critics, bigots, anyone who thinks being "politically correct" is a drag, any utterers of the words "politically correct" full end stop, jerks who don't listen when you talk—they are going to be even less attentive going-at-it-wise, your friends' partners unless you're all aware of and into that scenario, dudes who NEED you to know that they are feminists, white people who NEED you to know they advocate for people of color and/or "don't see race," anyone who makes fun of other people in a way reliant on the "teasing" part over the loving part (those elements are at their best when they're given equal, or close to equal, weight), male improv students, self-identified "philosophers," those who condescend, hashtag enthusiasts (unless that's for a cause or event), "truthers" of all stripes, hosts of the radio.

This is all highly subjective. You can obviously fuck, or not, any of these people at will, and you don't even have to like them to do that. I often hear arguments that hate-sex is some of the best sex out there, but I prefer to put on a one-act with someone of whom I am actually fond, in which we get vicious and violent while we're being physical, then are able to good-naturedly kid and kiss about it instead of parting ways in silent fury and derision. (Let me reiterate: Fucking DJs is a doomed way to spend your time.)

Some Notes on Grooming

You are under no obligation to present your body in any standardized model for sexiness. However: This is not a call to action against Big Soap. As a demonstration of respect toward your partners/insurance you'll have them to begin with, you DO have to make sure your zones are clean and smell *at least* neutral. What will improve your and a partner's time together is making sure you look hot in as close to the way you do inside your own head—on your best days—as you can muster. When my mettle is up, my lipstick is shadowy velvet, and my hair doesn't look like a post-pillow-friction tumbleweed *before* I get in bed, I'm liable to relax and mentally dedicate myself to what I'm doing with my body and how that feels, not how it looks. Conversely, if you could grease a baking sheet on my forehead and my teeth smell, you can bet that I'm fretting, which detracts from my ability to keep my mind on how my and my co-person's bodies feel. (Morning sex = not my favorite.)

My self-styled grossness is never as bad as I think it is, even when I'm SURE it is. If a person is having sex with you, it's probable that they do not share in your perception of yourself as half-beast-at-least. The trick to avoiding that head trap: Making sure you're aesthetically comfortable, whatever that means for you... but not stressing out over every! Last! Detail! Follow this rule: You are allowed to look in the mirror exactly twice, maximum, even in private, on a date.

The best ways to jazz up your sexual fitness, which is incontestable and inborn, is to be, in some way of your personal choosing, distinctive in your sartorial/outwardly formations. Go ahead and rise to *Tha Krazy Ol' Media*'s expectations about what you should slather and drape on yourself if you genuinely get a kick out of that, as I often do. There's no joy in conforming to gendered stereotypes of appearance because you're suffering under the misconception that following those tiresome codes to the letter is the only way you'll ever turn a partner on. Decorate yourself in modes super-feminine or -masculine if you like to do that, or you're probably better off not doing it at all. Your date is, let's hope, not judging you via a rubric that looks suspiciously like the "Fitness" section of a magazine display rack, but asserting that they are right to be doing that. Be complicit in someone essentializing you only if you're aware of and okay with/have your own reasons for that. Stay conscious of it either way.

When you personify ownership over and happiness with your body, even if you aren't 100 percent convinced of it in all moments, it grants your partner an improved likelihood of doing the same. You're less likely to set off another person's anxious review of their own zones for unworthiness. Confidence can be unnerving to some people, but I'm not really trying to get it in with anyone who needs me to feel unsure of my sexual aptitude as a result of worrying that my face might suck (and not in the crude way that syntax suggests, either). I used to become disruptively nervous if a comely person I was taking the clothes off of projected the opposite, and instead seemed ill at ease. This was before I figured out that even the most modelesque among the human race occasionally feel like lukewarm roadkill about their outfits, hairstyles, and bodies, so I could not yet identify the motivations behind when, say, they suddenly got quiet or started stammering. *Did some aspect of me disarm or dismay them?* I thought. *Is it because my face is a gigantic problem with inadequately-velveteen lipstick on it???* No! They were *also* petrified! The minute insecurities I fretted over seem so cyclical and useless when I could have crawled outside my head, quit trying to look sexy, and focused on the fact that the other person did. Appreciation is *also* usually a reciprocal act. Have you ever heard of "mirroring"? It's when, if a person likes someone with whom they're interacting, they unwittingly mimic their stances and poses. Making a nonverbal show of "good self-esteem" by not perceptibly loathing your appearance is no exception: Though it might feel like the flimsiest of shams at first, that grace is palpable, and so, communicable. "We are what we pretend to be," quoth Ernest Hemingway. The rest of that particular excerpt, if I recall, has gone missing somehow, but I believe it continued, "... and imitation is a form of self-flattery that will totally find you up to your eyeballs in vacant condom wrappers if you do it convincingly."

Another reason to shower today: If you're not bugging out over your appearance, you are tacitly confirming your agreement with your partner re: your being a sex-worthy person—and that they're a superb decision-maker for putting their skin in close proximity to yours, which feels good for all parties involved.

SHAVE, OR DON'T

There's something sexy, in a highly sweet and even goofy way, about premeditated pubic-hair grooming. You kind of can't beat making it with somebody for the first time and discovering that they were so eager and anticipatory that they trimmed their sub-equatorial zones into a discernible shape, or putting your hand down some gorgeous individual's pants and feeling the one true manifestation of the word "intent": a landing strip or other topiary that is a hair-oglyph translating to, "I am here to fuck you and I wanted you to know it." I don't care about how anybody's pubic hair looks except my own (a frustrating/hot conundrum: I prefer not to intervene with my bush, but getting head feels better sans pubes). Some people prefer pubic hair styled one way or another—and pornography suggests that people don't want to have sex with others of their kind whose genitals aren't those poreless, hairless blanknesses you see on mannequins, except with deeper tans—but you don't much have to worry about that unless you'd like to, which I sometimes do if I'm into somebody a lot in the aforementioned anticipatory way. The thing here is that *nobody* is going to jerk their head/hands/other appendages away from you if they notice that you do or don't have hair on some recently unclothed part of you—and if they did, you'd be spared some similarly unimaginative sex, so you'd win anyway.

The only exception to this rule is if you choose both not to depilate AND forgo a daily shower—scent clings to hair. (Even so: There are some people out there who are fetishistically into olfactory rankness. I love the smell of neglected armpits a ton, so I can relate to a lesser extent.)

Don't Be a Douche

If you own douche, aka a type of vaginal hygiene product, trash it immediately. That snake oil does the opposite of what it advertises, plus is required by law to be packaged in the most offensively corny ways possible. My anatomy is not a season or weather event, and I'm not sure what's *breezy* about giving yourself an increased risk of infection with the aid of pale slime that smells like rotted puberty. The powdery, chemical, and fundamentally shame-based odor of vaginal douche is almost as loathsome as its purported use. Not to sound like a zenergetic dipstick with morality-based dietary restrictions (even though I am), but *vaginas are naturally self-cleaning, sister,* and using special "washes" on your trim bungles that hygienic process. If you mess with the system, the system malfunctions, and although it sounds like I'm talking about a hard drive or something, this means, here, that you stop your body from working the only way it knows how to and leave it more vulnerable to bacterial contamination, which can lead to discomfort and infections. So springy and fresh!!!

YOUR WEIGHT DOESN'T
MATTER

Commenting on a person's weight or gender (e.g., in the latter case, making any remark that ends, "...for a boy/girl"), regardless of your intentions, is not a compliment. The rule of talking about other people's bodies: Unless you're saying something that, under an X-ray, breaks down to the elemental structure of "You look amazing," you shouldn't be saying anything. Last year, I lost a bunch of weight due to emotional stress. Initially, I was worried that my gauntness was going to lead people to classify me as "unhinged" or "unhealthy"—which are two bifurcations of the same root idea, that someone has a medical condition, but are not necessarily one identical fact. (This nervousness probably stemmed from the fact that both were totally true for me at the time.) I did find that others couldn't seem to stop being twerps about my shaved-down form, but it was because they lauded it, which was far worse for me. One night, three different jackhole acquaintances at a single "fashion party" effused over my weight, saying, "You're so skinny now! You used to be so *big*! You look gorgeous!" I've had pretty severe body issues throughout my life and have had to learn to shred through and past them, so I knew that this was cruddy and intrusive. I told each of them that I didn't think what they were saying was in any way flattering, but it still made me feel tangled-up about my value as a person in relation to my weight. Like, *I just came here to do tequila shots and maybe instigate a dance contest with a male model, and now I'm wondering how many calories I just nipped off of a toothpick when I downed that teensy passed appetizer, aka the one thing I ate today.* Maybe calm down with that.

(A bonus and so stunningly unexpected moral of this story: People who employ children as coatracks for the clothing of adult bodies are by and large vapid jackals, and part of how you can tell is because they scrutinize the bodies of others, and if that weren't harsh enough, they do it out loud.)

Later that night, I brought home a persistent club promoter (baaaaad mistake number one, but whatever). I had known him a few years back when I was a "professional" nightlife hostess, aka when I was skint and was paid to say "Hi there!! I'm Amy Rose and this is my party! Are you having fun?!" then go about my usual way of licking salt and limes and cheating my way to the top of the dance-off bracket. (Just get on the floor and twist your legs around dramatically and you win. You're welcome.)

After that dude and I boned, he made a belabored point of telling me how "crazy" it was that I was "so thin" now. "Your boobs used to be so big that it looked uncomfortable for you. You look *much* better" = A REAL THING THAT CAME OUT OF HIS MOUTH! About extreme weight loss that was based in poor health!

I was incensed. I had had my fill of being gawped at, heft-or-lack-thereof-wise. I read him the riot act, telling him it was totally impolite of him to talk to me like that, and could he please just keep any unwelcome commentary in that vein to himself? "All I meant was that you look really pretty...and skinny!" OH. All I mean is, there's the door, wad.

Be similarly unwavering with anyone who tries to tell you something contrary to your good looks.

WELCOME HOME

Including even Graceland, the myriad Taco Bell outposts across the nation, and the Musée d'Orsay in Paris, my bedroom is my favorite place on earth. I have lived here for five years, and it is the only place I've ever felt was my secure, for-sure home. Upon moving in, I spangled it thickly with tons of the beloved trash I'd collected prior (mementos like sea glass, old playing cards, faded paper wristbands, etc.). Now, I can see everything I consider important, meaningful, beautiful, and/or cool tacked up right on the walls—or, let's be realistic, pinned and mounted with Band-Aids or some political button reading, like, "SOCIALISM IS FOR EVERYONE" from my IDEALISTIC UNDERGRAD DAZE (hee—like I don't still feel that way, what with that implied *maturity* and *distance*). These adhesive methods are indicative of my general attitude toward home decor: My apartment isn't remarkable because it's tastefully organized, kitted out with even tangentially matching furniture, or otherwise aesthetically astounding. I have no idea how interior design works. Or maybe, thanks to my Band-Aids, I'm an iconoclastic master of the medium? Still deciding, but either way, I love my home because posting up on my bed feels like hanging out inside the antechamber of my brain.

My brain is sometimes a mess, though. When I'm working fifteen-hour days, my room reflects that: My dresser upchucks clothing onto the floor; errant fake eyelashes snar into tumbleweeds; rugs become thatched with hair extensions; my bed develops osteoporosis under the burden of ten thousand volumes of pompous New York School poetry. I'm not assigning too much of a stigma to that state of upheaval—it's just that, when your sheets are cram-packed with bar matchbooks and matching faux-fur separates, there's barely room to slot your *own* body, let alone another person's, in the spaces between all that flotsam.

If I were one of those plush dolls of a children's television character that warbles out a signature witticism when you pull a cord on its back, a strong contender for my catchphrase would be, "How about we go to yours?" (This is one of the multitudinous reasons why I will not be nominated for a Kids' Choice Award in this or any lifetime. The existence of this book is another.) It would be disingenuous to say that my reservations about extending visitation rights to hot young things—or hot middle-aged things, on occasion—my perversion knows no upper-age limitation—come solely from a *Cathy*-comic-esque feeling, to the tune of, "ACK! MY MANY, MANY DAIRY-SOILED PAJAMA TOPS ARE STREWN OVER MY SNOOPY HUMIDIFIER!

I'M A SEXLESS BARNACLE!" My apprehension comes instead from being cagey about showing people EXACTLY ALL OF WHO I AM RIGHT AWAY. (I know; *I am the only human being who has ever felt this way.*)

My bedroom, in its striking resemblance to my mind-piece, reveals me pretty handily. While its singularity is why I find it such a superlative place to hang out, it's also what used to make me bridle re: ushering in any old dreamboat on a whim—although I've involved myself with a great many sexual teammates during my stay, for a while, I brought them home only if I was certain I'd never see them again, and often not even then. My thinking went, *I don't need some gorgeous dolt treading all over the precious garbage-confetti of my life with muddy Vans on.* I'd rather create a mental Dewey decimal system of *their* bookshelves (or, if they're like me, library-duvet). You know—the kind where a person treats your books as a syllabus for divining what you're *really like*. I trust that most people exercise diplomacy in this regard— or, I hope they do, since trying to fix a person in place according to their tastes will give you an impression of their character that's tenuous at best, plus who cares—yet I'm still not always thrilled about a new acquaintance apprising the parameters of *how* comprehensive my library of alternative comics from the 1980s is. Not because I'm ashamed of what I like—the opposite! I'm *ferociously* proprietary when it comes to my brain and home.

I'm learning to unseal my cranial mausoleum. I'm a polite guest who will secretly use your hairbrush only A LITTLE, but even so, why should I impose upon others without ever expecting to be imposed upon myself? (Oh, because I'm giving them head. It's actually not the BIGGEST etiquette-based crime to swing by your partner's estate on the regular, but whatever—I've got to be less shy, or else recede into hermitry for good.) In order to ameliorate my *Life in Hell*–based anxieties, I've developed the following techniques for welcoming houseguests with whom I'm looking to catch some play instead of baldly lying all like, "Let's keep the lights off—yes, my 'body' 'insecurity' is through the roof. MAN, are these calves ever c-crummy," so they don't see that I have not one but FOUR Smiths posters up and (correctly) run screaming. I'd much rather gaze upon whatever piece of tail I've granted visitation rights than feign meekness because I'm an egregiously private weirdo.

Though I live mostly alone (this book is basically dedicated to my roommate's girlfriend, the person to whom he should *really* be paying rent—big ups, Emily, for unwittingly aiding and abetting in my sexual fulfillment), and you might take up residence in a shared loft, apartment, or centuries-old Edwardian castle (look, I don't know you, dude, so why not let me imagine you're some regal archduke or whatever?), I'm confident that, like socialism, this guide will be beneficial to just about everyone. (New slogan idea: "END THE FED / GET IN MY BED." Why am I not yet the president?) In terms of creating an "inviting atmosphere" with my home decor, impasto-ing a living space with babes has turned out to surpass using even the most anticapitalist of button propaganda when it comes to decorative fixtures! Since they populate my DEEPEST OF INTERIOR THOUGHTS AND TASTES as much as all the other lovely junk I have pinned/bandaged up, it's only in keeping with my overarching design strategy.

Draw those blinds, hide that humidifier AND the stylish Peanuts flannel it's wearing, and take a deep breath, my brothers and sisters in arms: We're having a house party tonight, and the guest list is "freaks only"—which just beat out my previous Amy Rose Doll slogan by a minute mile...but is still pretty unfit for children's network programming.

CLEANLINESS IS NEXT TO BODLINESS

My home is, on occasion, piled high with refuse. You get it: We exult in our careers (and look great doing it! HAH, I'm wearing two towels as a bikini right now), are busy, and/or are beholden to excessive sloth! All three are true of my situation. But if the bastion of human sexuality just texted you, "I'd love to see you; how about I come over in 30?" great job on landing a dreamboat who uses a semicolon in casual communication, seriously, and HOLY SHIT, you have a graveyard of tallboys and magazines and broken sunglasses for carpeting. IS THAT A LIVING PIGEON IN THE CORNER, DUDE? Looks like it's time for another round of...HIDE! THAT! GARBAGE! *[studio audience whips itself into a near-to-deafening frenzy]*

Hide! That! Garbage

A fake quiz show I just invented to make a cleaning spree seem like less of the frightful punishment we all know it is

Round One: Trashcatcher! This is like when contestants have to snatch money out of the air as it precipitates inside a little booth, but *so much worse*. Have two colors of garbage bags on hand to separate actual rubbish from the clutter you just need to stash real quick-like. Pack your various litter/belongings in these, respectively, and hurl them into a closet to deal with at some distant point after you've had ten zillion orgazmzzz—your main priority, doye. Verify that the following items are properly concealed: visibly cashed dirty underwear; condom wrappers; Post-its with self-affirming messages written on them in manic penmanship ("YOU ARE A WORTHY CHILD OF THE SUN" = not great to explain, in terms of pillow talk, or also ever, at any other time); empty champagne cans; old copies of *Hustler* (again, you are a stranger to me and I don't know your tastes, ya depraved archduke).

Round Two: Obstacle Recourse! Light a candle and open a window. Stuff all available dresser drawers with whatever non-scuzzy possessions are taking up the most surface area. DO

NOT PAUSE TO ORGANIZE. YOU DO NOT HAVE TIME. Throw all remaining stray clothes underneath your bed and excavate them later (this goes for any other floor-eating lumps of stuff you aren't relegating to plastic-bag purgatory, too). Empty the litter box, if applicable. Make your bed and flip over its top layer if you recently ate, painted, or bled on it. Wipe down surfaces.

Round Three: Bone Zone Bonus Bonanza! Put your books in your bookshelf or stack them in a corner, turning spine-in any volumes that are too cornily 1980s or whatever your version of pulpy Bret Easton Ellis dross is, as well as titles in any way similar to *You Are a Worthy Child of the Sun: A Guide to Manifesting Your Inner Zenergy*, and also, probably, this book. Make sure you have at least two clean drinking glasses at the ready, then rinse the rest of the dirty dishes and stash them in the oven. FEBREZE. Put on anodyne, affable music, like *The Essential Sly and the Family Stone* or any De La Soul megamix, so you don't have to parse the annals of your music library upon the person's arrival.

Dag: This well-groomed manse was hiding underneath the novelty state keychain collection you spilled two weeks ago, then forgot about, *this whole time*?

What about YOU, darling thing? How are you looking/smelling? My guess is, "Great—yo, what a babe, get over here," but if you happen to have spent the day playing Game Boy in a fragrant broth of your own sweat heretofore until now, let's blitz. In order:

• Take off your clothes and stuff them under the bed or in a closet. As you do this, think about how much fun it's going to be to disrobe again in the next little while—you know, without all the sessility-based shame.

• Twitch your nose at your charmpits. Do they smell like they're about to ferment? If you waver on whether or not they might be terrible, wash those cesspools in the sink, and put on deodorant, for cripes' sake.

• Apply perfume or cologne if you're not already wearing it. Rather than hosing yourself down with fragrance at point-blank range, which unsubtly screams, "I KNEW YOU WERE COMING BY TO INHALE MY EXTERNALITIES FROM CLOSE RANGE IN A FUCK-BASED CAPACITY," spritz *once* into the air in front of you from a fully extended arm's length and walk through the mist in the buff. This gives you more of a "I happen to smell like a seraph who exudes a natural air of jasmine and verbena" type effect. (Side note: What even is verbena? The world may never know.)

• Strap on some clean underwear that's free of holes and stains. The newer, the better—every time I denude in front of someone and have to strip off the threadbare Hello Kitty panties that once belonged to my seventh-grade girlfriend and have a bush-revealing hole in the whiskers, I cross my eyes at the heavens, like, *How dare you.* If you wear bras, make sure this one is intact—dryer-withered underwire is an all-around bummer.

• Put on an outfit that's been recently laundered and is easy to take off. No weirdo zippers or buttons, please! Who's ever trying to make/hear the "joke" that goes, "Ha-ha, I'm out of practice, I guess," as a maker-out fumbles with inexplicable chest snaps? Not you, not me, not anyone.

• If your hair is dirty, sprinkle the smallest amount of baby powder in your hands and run them all up throughout that grease trap. If it's long and a mess, tie it back.

• Brush your chops, put on makeup if you like it, and curl your lip at the bathroom mirror: You look eminently bangable.

SETTING A MOOD

Let's say you have plenty of time and don't have to invent a panicked game show to calm yourself down. Let's say you aren't even a messy person, and instead have a non-figurative carpet that matches your non-figurative drapes. (And prefab bad, smutty jokes at the ready to go with them.) There are plenty of accents to help elevate that already-august sense of home decor to one that is tastefully nasty! Okay, let's do it, here is the list:

- Grapeseed oil
- *Now! That's What I Call Music 14*
- An indoor hammock
- An assortment of personalized Christmas stockings (year-round; none bearing your own name)
- A prominently displayed collection of Happy Meal Beanie Babies
- A miniature gong, or, even better, two

Combine and delight, my profligate sex fiends.

For real: You don't need any material goods to leave an indelible impression. There are, however, certain considerations about what's worth having on hand, and I promise they have nothing to do with the holiday season or a compilation including the works of Aaron Carter. In addition to the regular safe-sex necessities you do (and you DO) have close at hand, there are a handful of practical objects you should consider, if you're not too busy trying not to lose miserably at *Hide! That! Garbage!*

Chief among these are the provisions based in the kind of foresight that further verifies you as a suave person who knows their every movement twelve steps before it happens. The beauty of providing this kind of toolkit is that it makes you look so put-together because it's solely about anticipating the needs and comfort of your guest, which is pretty easy, seeing as they're baseline the same as your own. The basics you should have readily at hand:

- A clean towel, should your person want to rinse or otherwise blot themselves off after consummating
- Water (or, preferably, seltzer), because sex requires exertion, and if you're incorporating oral, making sure no one gets cotton mouth will make it more enjoyable
- A tissue box or paper towels, for everything

It's dreamy to have a post-sex uniform at the ready, too. I like leotards, knee-length tube socks, and roller-disco cotton gym shorts, but clean white T-shirts, hoodies, and boxers look good on everyone. Oh my god, imagine if you wore a comely robe? What are you, a deity? Of sex??? Yes, please wear a robe. (As long as it's not a sexless terrycloth BATHrobe.)

ROOMMATING PATTERNS

If you have roommates, tell them the fuck-situation, and ask them to please make themselves scarce—or, even better, to fuck-situation off for a while. (Big ups to Emily, again, for making this conversation moot. You really hold it down, dude.) It's not the end of the world if your houseguest has to shake hands with a person unrelated to your entanglement in order to earn the grand prize of stripping you down in your bedroom, but if I had a roommate whom I didn't like or who was overly inquisitive—to my date or to ME about my date later on—I'd circumvent those conversations as much as possible.

Your roommate is under no mandate to oblige you—it's their home, too—but it's helpful if you have an agreement in place where they know you'll evacuate when they have guests. If you reciprocate departures, your roommate will likely be cool about it, and then you can scream the loudest, weirdest shit you can think of while you're getting down, if you're so inclined, without fear of being overheard: "MARS IS A BIG HOAX!" "WINTER IS CAN-CELED!" "ATTENTION, RESPECTED UNITED NATIONS COLLEAGUES: THIS IS THE FILTHIEST MOMENT OF MY LIFE."

If those with whom you live are within earshot: Play music loudly enough to muffle any pillow talk/staccato porn-moans, but not so loud that your housemate is inclined to knock and ask you to pipe down in there, already.

Casanova's Breakfast Buffet

Once upon a time, I was boning this one guy whom I thought was such a sophist—he wore impressive, but not loudly expensive-looking, shoes and put me on to the Federico García Lorca essay "In Search of Duende." What confirmed his elegance was the breakfast he served me when I woke up at his place for the first time. To the end of helping you leave a similarly gracious impression on your own houseguests, I've remorselessly jacked his menu and reproduced it here.

This meal has a tiny element of effort to it, but only so far as that you're making an egg. It's very casual, as in, yogurt in a bowl with sliced produce/mixers on the side, like a fit person who leads their life with more intent than I do. The key is the three beverages—they hydrate, brighten up, and revivify you in case you want to have early-bird special sex.

The grocery list, in total, will cost you $20 or less unless you get unnecessarily upscale ingredients (and this cost is lower if you already have some of what it comprises in the house, which you will), is vegetarian, and takes under ten minutes to make, no matter how hungover you are.

What you'll need:

- Greek yogurt
- Toast
- Jam
- Strawberries
- Macadamia nuts
- Coffee
- Grapefruit juice
- San Pellegrino or other seltzer (but Pelly is best)
- An egg

How to lay it out most appealingly:

On a clean table, place the stuff that comes in jars and plastic packages, aka the jam, nuts, and berries, into three small

(continued)

bowls, each with spoons, and put it by a bowl of the yogurt. Fold a napkin (or a paper towel, if, like me, you can't be knackered with more than one kind of disposable cloth in your kitchen) next to that, and set utensils on it. Fry the egg, toast the toast, and plate them. Finish the spread with a glass for each beverage.

The most crucial ingredient to a debonair breakfast: Do not ask if your guest is hungry. Assemble the food, lay it out, and nonverbally convey, "Eat it or not; I'm honestly too busy reading Lorca to care." It's kind and sexy. Save for the toast and egg, you can simply put it away if they don't want it.

WHATTA DISH

Have a signature seduction snack! I find that even the most lax hookups appreciate being offered a Fruit Roll-Up, vodka soda, prosecco, handful of blueberries, or ice-cream sandwich varietal upon arrival at my home. These cover all the bases of people you might be sleeping with: hot, overgrown moron with a heart of gold; super-fun dilettante alcoholic; person who owns a mountain bike or feasibly could (check for a lanyard on their belt loop; this has the double utility of telling you all you need to know about the state of their pubic hair in advance); and spouse material.

Your shopping cart: something packed with sugar and artificial everything, something mind-altering to take the edge off, something where the recipient will be like, "My, my—now here's a person who snacks on a known source of antioxidants for PLEASURE, because they LIKE IT? Goodness, I didn't know I could *become* so sprung," and more more more sucrose sugar sugar!!! You can customize this at will—my only gentle warning is to shy away from any processed corn snack that leaves a dusting of easily communicable orange moss on your fingers and tongue, unless that's a deliberate fetish you have.

One of the most impressed faces I have ever seen on a partner was pulled when, on my way to the shower, I offered him one of the abundance of Take 5 bars I keep in my freezer at all times. He looked at me in wonderment and said, "You know this is like a parody of a perfect sexual encounter, right? You are *really* offering me a candy bar after we came at the same time?"

The best part: Even if you don't get laid, all of these comestibles taste just as good if you're eating them while post-up with your newspaper by yourself, morning after or nah—especially the ice-cream sandwiches, Take 5s, and vodka. Aren't you glad you've created such a mature and welcoming home?

PART II

Protect Me from What I Want

The above chapter title, from artist Jenny Holzer, extends to the body as usefully as it does to the heart. I mostly regard sex as a means, not an end: I am discussing all this belt-loop notching with regards to sex as recreation, not procreation. The foundation of ensuring agency within this for yourself and others is accounting for, and doing your best to dramatically reduce, the risk of facing down any long-term life alterations as a result of getting laid. However airtight your consent and methods of protection, there's no impermeable way to make sure that you or your partner won't surface from bed with a new medical diagnosis, including "pregnant as hell."

Preventing those conditions is easier than it has ever been. We are lucky enough to live in a time when prophylactics are not only readily available, but so profuse as to come in varieties that sound like the cocktail menu at a chain restaurant in the mall (although I will neither make love with nor drink anything branded as "Twizted Cherry Passion…Flavored For Her," thank you very much).

Condoms, the main barrier method of birth control, are crucial if you want to twizt your passions with respect to penetration. There are also plenty of other preventative measures when it comes to the interlacing of your sexual health with a person's that includes STIs while still enjoying your time together. (If you have one of these under your belt already, you already know that it doesn't preclude all sexual caprice, forever.)

Let me reiterate, since informing yourself thoroughly about sexual health is capital: I'm not a doctor, as far as I know. I'm a woman who delights in maintaining my confidence that I can engage in frottage with the whole sequence of the cosmos and remain relatively unscathed, and I do my research. Here's a distilled version of what I know—I encourage you to augment it with further reading.

EVERYTHING'S UNDER CONTROL

My condom policy is thus: It's not one person's "responsibility" to provide foils. With a reasonable margin for forgetfulness, the occasional lean times between paychex, and extenuating circumstances like "the store's closed and I'm rolling up to your spot at 3 a.m. after agreeing to meet a whim that you just texted me you'd had," every person anticipating imminent coitus is obligated to furnish protection, unless you're a couple with a shared econodom-box in your co-owned nightstand.

Discovering you're out of stock, condom-wise, just as you're reaching to use one can lead to a ruthless urgency to throw on pants and procure some at the store across the street that I find very hot. More often, it's tedious and mood-slackening to have to wait on a person's bed all like, *It's been five minutes and I'm getting restless—can I reach for my phone without sacrificing the mood entirely?* Plus, not everyone makes their home opposite a bodega . . . which, how do you even survive without one? I can't fathom having to prepare for life before it happens, you upstanding models of organization.

My solution, when my bedroom became a naked waiting room one too many times, was to treat condoms like other parts of my grocery list: *paper towels, dish soap, condoms, toothpaste.* Like everything else accounted for here, condoms are necessary maintainers of your upkeep that you will never overstock, since you'll need them in perpetuity. If this kills a certain spirit for you, if you are besotted with the sheer intentionality of going to the store and buying prophylactics before meeting someone you think is supersexy, go forth with your ritual. That errand feels mad nice. (Just please remember to make it.)

Now that you have a bounty of condoms and aren't afraid to use them, let's talk about a situation that reverses the latter idea. Did your condom just break?! Don't panic. Yes, a teeny fissure in a thin disc of rubber instantly set off a chain of headaches with which you'll have to contend, and that's unfortunate. If you need to freak all the way out about it, I exhort you to wait, because you have more immediate priorities, and zeroing in on the pragmatic ways to make this situation suck less, instead of lamenting its misfortune, works formidably in your favor—as it would in any luckless scenario, latex-based or nah.

Did the person with the penis ejaculate before this wrenching discovery was made? If yes: Do not try to flush the offending substance out with water. There's no way to "wash" come out once it's made genital contact, and you need to focus on more productive steps away from accidental parenthood.

Emergency contraception is low-cost and simple to buy (at least if you live in America). You can cop it at most pharmacies and drugstores that stock other kinds of over-the-counter medicines, and some brands cost as little as ten bucks per. If you can't make it to the store by the next day, it's okay—you have up to three days to take pills with the active ingredient of progestin. Ones that utilize other kinds of hormones can be effective for up to five days, too, if you're willing to pay more. But, honestly, if you're able to go take care of this right away and *choose* not to: What are you actually doing? What schedule obligations are more important than making sure you don't have to be responsible for at least a surgery and at most a human life?

It's not a brilliant idea to make a regular practice of taking hormonal modifiers, which is what most morning-after pills are, since they can make you sick. Despite certain media chatter, there's not a large faction of sexually active people using the morning-after pill as a primary form of birth control for this reason. That is fabulist political nonsense that ignores the realities that condoms are far thriftier and don't make their customers want to ralph.

The availability and destigmatization of emergency contraceptives is a societal boon, since accidents frequently warrant their name, and it's not just okay, but smart and necessary, to use the morning-after pill in the times for which it was invented to help you and your partner.

STANDARDIZED TESTING

Get tested for sexually transmitted infections (STIs) once or twice a year, even if you've been thoughtful about protection. There's not much need to check in with a doctor or clinic if you've maintained the same sexual partner or partners from the last time you peed in a cup (as long as you are POSITIVE that you two are monogamous), those who run around more might like to go at least once a year, barring any unforeseen prophylactic mishaps. I don't subscribe to going after *each and every partner no matter if you kept things tightly wrapped*. It colors sex with a high degree of unnecessary panic—the fear of *being punished by a plague for the dreadful sin of having an orgasm* feels melodramatic, and also like it comes from a few centuries before birth control rose to the massive popularity it enjoys today. However, I understand that for many people, the impetus to check up on everything, every time, is meant to ameliorate anxiety that they've jeopardized their well-being by exposing themselves to below-the-belt frogs and locusts. If that's what you need to do in order to feel responsible and healthy, I not only encourage, but demand, that you do it. Your health is yours to dictate.

When you DO go get tested, at whatever volume you do that, you can go to either your regular physician's office or a sexual health–focused clinic like Planned Parenthood. There's no one all-encompassing screening for each and every STI running rampant through the sheets, so you have a short conversation with a medical professional about what-all you've been up to, and they determine what diagnoses to test for. They ask you things about birth control, doye, but also inquire about more pointed parts of your sexuality—what body parts are involved when you bone, the genders of the people whom you bone, and so forth. If you don't identify along the straight-and-narrow hetero spectrum of sexuality or gender identity, it can be assuring to have your tests conducted by a medical practitioner whom you know will treat you with respect and knowledge of non-hetero *eros*. You likely know that, like any other person, some doctors have inflexible, gross biases and prejudices about non-binary *livin' and lustin'*. Here are a few good resources to help you locate practitioners minus these flaws:

Planned Parenthood
Mayo Clinic
The Door

As I mentioned: Even if you're taking another form of birth control and are having monogamous sex with someone you trust, you honestly cannot know if they're "safe" unless they furnish the proper paperwork. I'm not big on quizzing people, but it can be fun to *get tested together*. It isn't as awkward or accusatory as it sounds! A dude of yore and I wanted to go latex-free, but we each wanted to show the other that that was a solid idea, STI-wise. We decided to make some sort of romantic display of it, I guess, by demonstrating that we'd accept whatever new results we learned of, or didn't, as long as we found out and accounted for them together. Filled with loving resolve and determined to bareback it, we embarked on our modern, free-lovin' errand, feeling mad adult and responsible and sexually in control. Nothing makes you feel like a person who acts with intelligent, capable intent like taking care of your body, so it's pretty attractive to observe someone else as they do that.

Neither my partner nor I anticipated any future-altering results (outside the more figurative one of a renewed and strengthened bond of trust shared by hopeful young lovers…nauseating, I know). Still, I can never help thinking, *What if?* in waiting rooms. It doesn't matter if I couldn't even manage to convincingly invent a symptom with the entire medical internet as my research assistant. Prior to a test, part of me upholds a worrisome conviction of some latent sickness patiently filing its nails in my bloodstream.

In the waiting room, and not for the first time, my cohort and I talked about what might happen if one of us had an STI.

"Will you still want to jump my bones if I somehow have whooping crotch?" I asked.

"What? Do you mean herpes? Whatever you're talking about: Yeah, as long as you keep track of your outbreaks and we always use condoms. And you don't have anything, but if you do, it would take way more to keep me off of you."

Improbably, I was teetering on the brink of foreplay in the sterile offices of a sexual-malady depot, but I managed to keep it together for decorum's sake.

"Oh! *Ahem. [crosses legs tightly in self-discipline]* S-same. Even if you have an STI that I'm not into adopting as my very own, I'll find other ways to make you come, and you could still give me incredible head, like usual."

STIS, BY THE BY

Having no personal experience with STIs, I have no advice about their care and keeping. It's not my job to tell you that stuff. (Well, hold on. Let me pretend I took the Hippocratic oath just this once—"I swear on the game Hungry Hungry Hippos or whatever, thanks for letting me be a doctor now.") What doctors don't always have an opinion about, and on which I certainly do: How to tell someone you want to bone that you have a sexual health condition, and how to receive that news respectfully.

I know a fleet of people with herpes or other STIs—and some of them are among my most sexually conservative friends and loved ones, because having a communicable bodily medical condition can stem from arbitrary bad luck. How they break the news to partners is usually adapted to each person, but the wide commonality seems to be this: When you're disclosing what you have, do it prior to your first bone-a-thon, and do it with levity.

You can approach your medical status in a roundabout way by relaying an anecdote about a time an alarmist person in your life misunderstood the implications of your STI and saying, "I know this is the first you're hearing about this, by the way, and we can talk about it whenever you want." Or you can be direct and frank, like the person who paused and told me he had HPV when we were kissing all up on each other. As long as you say SOME-THING, you are doing the right thing. Go with whatever feels most natural and comfortable.

The person on the receiving end might not know much about your condition, and will likely have questions for you about it. Answer them, maintaining the cheery "This aspect of my medical history doesn't spell grim doom for my entire sexual future and is just a part of my life!" tone that you will keep in place throughout this conversation. They have the right to do whatever they feel is best for them—and it's not a commentary on your sexual fitness either way. I'm inclined to feel that if someone chooses not to find a compromising position (in all ways) that avoids contact with the affected areas, they should be, if anyone, the ones in this encounter worried about being judged. But, again, everyone has the right to call the shots about their own bodies. If you're ever asked, in this way, to be your own anatomical referee: Don't be the horse's ass who bugs out when someone gives you medical news. Be calm and empathetic. (As ever.)

CAUTIONARY MEASURES

It's not stodgy or prim to defend/remove your fine ass from sexual goings-on if your emotional or bodily safety is ever at stake. This advice goes for all people, of all genders, about all people, of all genders. I know plenty of hulking straight dudes who have been taken advantage of by women, gay girls who have been preyed on by gay girls, and have heard stories firsthand about assault that took place between so many other permutations of identities out there. This is a concern for all people, not just women and non-binary people. (But it's particularly relevant to women and non-binary people, whom are not as legally well-protected or granted as much credibility as straight cis dudes.) Acknowledging this does not make you a pearls-clutching alarmist. I really and truly believe that most of the people you "get to know" over the course of a well-executed sexual career will be cool to you. It's *still* better to be thoroughly reassured that you're keeping your wits about you all the way through (especially if you're a woman, queer, and/or trans). If you do, you can go about your mission(ary) position) with even more confidence and ease.

There have been times when I didn't know how to functionally advocate for myself, but even if I had: Situations in which I have been hurt tend to arrange themselves in a sequence that looks preventable only in hindsight. I have no idea what I could have changed about them, but am certain that any sexual disrespect I've taken is not mine to feel guilty about.

At twenty-one, I was eager about the prospect of having sex with a few people during a five-day tropical vacation, but I didn't expect what I thought was a coup on the first night out: My sister Laura and I met twin brothers—fraternal, but the degree to which they were gorgeous was identical—at the bar off the casino. As they bought drinks and led us to the dance floor, Laura leaned over to me and whispered, "We've gotta keep an eye on these Suit Brothers," as if that weren't a priori OBVIO from the minute they Armani-Exchanged across our line of vision.

One was named Rafa and the other Juanpablo, a name spit as one fused word from the mouth of a sharper-featured, suaver iteration of his bro. JP landed a few sly compliments as we spoke—"You know? You look like you have a spotlight on you even though it is dark in here. Would you like to light up the beach with me?" (This is obviously too schmaltzified for life, but like I said: godlike face.) Since I was already wearing my bikini in the club because I believe in dressing for success in all moments, I accepted the invitation.

We strolled not to the shore—since hair, as we know, is not actually effulgent, it seemed risky to meander down to a blackened beach in another country with a strange Suit Brother, even for this unflappable wearer of bathing suits in the club. I suggested we opt for one of the well-lit pools on the resort grounds, which was shallow and featured an inlaid mosaic of stars. I boned him right there on that subaqueous cosmos. This might sound pretty Harlequin-novel, thus far in my story: a spontaneous encounter with a rakish, continental stranger in a luxury pool in a different country with mad stars both under my butt and above my head! It sure felt novelistic: I was so romantically self-possessed and free!

Then he punched me in the face.

The stars multiplied again from the impact. Before they dissipated, I had already hauled off and clocked him right back, and the velocity at which my fist connected with his geometric jaw surprised me, but not as much as it did him. Uncertain of what came next in this diversion from the story line, we froze.

"Why did you hit me like that? You didn't even ask!" he sputtered, running a chlorine-wet hand over his chin. "Funny—I know exactly the feeling, dude," I said flatly.

JP looked mortified as I continued: "Did you really think that was going to fly? You have to make sure it's okay with someone before you do that, fuckface, no matter how spontaneous and rough things seem." He apologized. I didn't.

Should something like this ever happen to you: If you feel endangered, or like what you're physically comfortable with has been dismissed in favor of the other person's pleasure, *get out of that situation.* If you told that person no, in any capacity, about something that they did anyway, you can report them to whatever authorities you can: police; security if you're in a place that has it; a league of friends-and-family street vigilantes.

Some of us don't feel that they can report sexual assault, and I understand that. The fucked-up thing about reporting sexual assault, violence, or rape is that, in some cases, those responsible for upholding the law will not help you, even if you report what happened "perfectly," which is a fallacy that means "within a certain time frame, and under certain conditions." If you can report without feeling dysfunctionally worse, persecuted, and/or scared, it's still worth doing: If nothing else, it most likely puts the grimehole who hurt you on official record as having this complaint against them, which will make it less difficult to nail this person if it should ever happen again, to you or someone else.

You are not obligated to traumatize yourself in order to "do the right thing" and alert the authorities if someone has done you harm. If you feel you'll be put at risk, or even just unsettled, if others know what happened, or if you're worried that, as is bitterly the case for many victims of sexual assault, your assailant's denial or even social reputation might be the one people are inclined to side with over your real account of what went down: You have the right to remain silent. And I'm sorry, and hope you can confide in someone who loves you, plus a good therapist, if you feel that would be helpful.

Someone doesn't have to hit you in order to make you feel unsafe or otherwise freaked out about sex, of course, and that lack of violence doesn't correspond to a lack of validity in terms of your gross feelings about what's happening. I was not made by dominant physical force to have non-consensual sex, the two times that's happened. (I have been pretty lucky, which is an amazing thing to say about being raped twice. "It was only twice! Gee, that's almost as good as winning the lottery that many times!")

Once, someone I trusted took advantage of me in my own home when I was supremely trashed. His best friend, my boyfriend, was asleep in our bed one room away. The other time, as a teenage person, I was berated into doing something I didn't want to. I "acquiesced" to that boyfriend's physical advances because I was stoned and found it cumbersome to keep repeating "no" and moving his hand off of, then out of, the fly of my jeans. I didn't consider it "real" rape because he wasn't aggressively forceful with me. No bruises? I must have wanted it after all, even though I verbally reprised over and over that I didn't. Everyone owes it to themselves to trust their feelings and decisions far more than that.

How can you tell if some malcontent's intentions for you are dangerous or don't account for you as an equal person? Well, sometimes you can't. There's no use, or logic, in beating yourself up in those cases: YEAH, YOU ARE HORRIBLE AND IN THE WRONG FOR NOT GUESSING THAT SOMETHING THAT IS USUALLY EXCITING AND WONDERFUL WAS GOING TO BE USED TO HURT YOU BY A CRETINOUS SPIT GLOB. Something to bellow from deep where I know it in the soles of my feet to the tiny split ends Alfalfa-ing off the top of my head right now: You are never accountable for another person's abuse of your trust. If something happens to you, the shame of that should only shackle the person who chose it.

While staying super-aware of what's going on might help reduce the risk of your being hurt, no amount of self-defense and -awareness is infallible. Protecting yourself doesn't extend only to deciding not to skip merrily down dark alleyways at 3 a.m. while high. (If you did decide to do that, you STILL wouldn't deserve to be hurt.) Sexual assault and rape, the majority of the time, are the work of someone the victim knows or is even close with. Recall how only one of those three times I was violated did I not know the person to be "a really good guy" or "my actual high school sweetheart of many years."

Still: Even if I sound like a super-herb, it's so important to try your best to look out for yourself even if the situations at hand (or junk) aren't palpably dangerous. This has meant that after returning from my island getaway, I behave like I'm being paid to be my own armed guard.

Please do not do what I did and blithely remain fixed on the arm of anyone trying to lead you to an isolated, indeterminate place, even if it's ostensibly a public one, for *at least* your first few encounters.

Of course that dude didn't want to have an oh-so-sensuous shore-side sand-everywhere tropical lover's tryst! If he had been considering my position at all in the slightest, he would have thought, *Man, it would be really predatory-seeming of me to ask her to a big, anonymous beach after dark when she's far from home and doesn't know me from Adam! Let me figure out someplace she'll feel safer.* I mean, I was able to come up with a less nebulous sexual landscape (or so I thought, but at least I had chosen it) in an instant after rejecting his first spot; plus, we were both with our siblings, whom we could have easily given the number of the room we were going to and told, "I'll check in by X time, and if I don't, come up." (This is exactly what Laura did with Suit Bro. #2, and she was fine.)

If you have to turn down the first place a person proposes that you two get risqué, that should wave an entire nation's supply of red flags at you. If you want to continue—maybe your companion is dense? It happens—tell them why you need to go somewhere you feel more comfortable and gauge their reaction: "[X PLACE] is too out of the way/dark/set apart from other spots for me. I'd rather do [X AMAZING-SOUNDING THING] someplace I know is okay."

If they say, "Of course—where do you want to go?" and honor your request without complaint... well, stay vigilant anyway. But I'd be a lot less worried than if the person protested, told you you were being uptight or to, like, "have some fun" or "just go with it" (ONLY DIRTBAGS STRING THOSE WORDS TOGETHER IN THAT ORDER WHILE PROPOSING SEX), or refused to go elsewhere. In those cases, I'd be out.

Should your intended safe spot be where you live: Exercise serious judgment about whom you bring home—this person now knows where to find you again. Are you okay with that? I usually am, but if I have some inkling that I shouldn't be, I wait until I can dispel it to invite a person over.

If you *welcome* a new acquaintance to pay a call, do all you can to make that person feel safe. For all they know, your closet is stuffed not with the overflow from your long-suffering hamper, but with your secret scalpel collection, organized in fastidious order from sharpest to "still terrifyingly sharp." Keep the lights on unless they ask that you turn them off, and don't close the door to your room without first locking down the absolute certainty that they're ready to take part in some private goings-on with you. And PUT AWAY YOUR MEDICAL INSTRUMENTS if you do for some reason have them, you fascinating lunatic.

If you're the visitor, follow my sister Laura's lead: Make sure you let a friend in on your whereabouts, including the address, if you don't know this dreamboat very well. Should something feel funny upon your arrival, text your friend that you're leaving by X time, then let them know when you make a break for it.

Home security isn't the last of your concerns—sexual violence can and does happen everywhere. Your gut will tell you if something seems untoward, and I try not to get too plastered to properly hear mine if I'm looking to get down. I never get together with a stranger when I'm too wasted to function otherwise, no exceptions—and anyone who would sleep with you when you're visibly *throwed* is probably not looking out for your best interests. If you're on the town with a friend, make them aware of this rule in case you can't be, via some encounter that goes something like, "YES OF COURSE I'D LIKE ANOTHER LONG ISLAND ICED TEA, FRANK. OH, SORRY—IT'S PETER, RIGHT, RIGHT." (I have been quoted thusly once or twice in the past, as I am nothing if not an excellent conversationalist in every moment.) When you try to abscond home with Frankenpeter or whomever you're into, your partner in crime will be there to remind you of the figurative KEEP OUT sign over your door instead.

WITHIN BOUNDS

Even when I haven't had a hunch that someone means me ill, I am my own warden when it comes to preventing people from unintentionally causing me discomfort—and I try to take care of the people I'm having sex with, too. You might not know what someone's history of abuse or trauma might be. It's imperative that you ask your partner, out loud, if some new act you're introducing into your physical hangout is okay with them. I don't expect people to do this for quotidian-seeming above-the-waist touching ALL THE TIME, but, I think the more you ask, the better. It doesn't have to slacken the fervidity of what's going down!

It's impossible to guess what a person might feel skittish about. Something you think is not only totally on the level, but also distinguishes you as an elevated prime sex master, could be fraught with the BAD kind of nostalgia for your partner.

You know how tons of people love it when someone plants one on their neck? When someone tries to kiss me there, it's possible that I'll recoil into brain-shivers and moribund thoughts because of some violence that was done to me there in the past. I have to be conscious of that and let the person literally necking with me know about it beforehand. Sound like a bummer? A worse one: NOT doing so, and having the person think that I am an oversensitive freakbag with a dented-up past as I squish myself away from them and into the wall.

For a while, I tried fibbing about why I wore an invisible caution-tape necklace. But when I told someone I was ticklish, I ran the risk of their testing that theory (in the cases they were monsters). Just imagine how well that went down! *Directness is best*. If I think someone is about to go for the throat, I steer them away and say, "Hey, everything you're doing feels amazing, but I just don't like being touched there. Try here instead," and traffic-control their hands or mouth to other vicinities. See how that keeps the pace of the hookup while ALSO making sure I'm not having a meltdown? Pretty sick, right?

When I'm asking others, I take a similar tack: "Would you like it if I did [X THING]?" I say this under my breath, with my eyes evenly connected to the other person's. Doesn't that seem like foreplay more than it does a reminder that many of us have had to endure condemnable bodily disrespect that scarred us forever??? Having tested this formulation many times over, I can tell you that it does.

Credit: Annie Mok

Credit: Annie Mok

On that "consent isn't sexy" tip: If you believe that's true, YA ACTUALLY DEAD WRONG. I so admire—and am turned on by—people who make a sturdy effort to make sure all's clear between us. It floods me with trust and warmth, which I usually like to express by tenderly mauling my partner however they like that best. When a person I like halts me at any point, even when it seems rubber-stamp-notarized that we're heading somewhere specific, and asks, "Is it okay if I [insert here]?" I am then positive that they are a good fuck. This is also true of when they let me in on what's not okay for them. If a person knows and cares enough about how to be good to their partners, it's all but guaranteed that equal devotion to making you feel A+ will be present in their efforts.

I make sure to sensually interrogate all my partners about what's permissible and what isn't, because I think many people don't feel comfortable bringing up their pasts on their own. If where and how people can touch you have their borders, you should let someone know what they are before they test them. If you two are close enough to fuck, you're close enough to tell each other how to do it, like how I offer up that my neck is a NO TRESPASSING area. It's unwise to expect everyone you sleep with to abide by your sexual bylaws if they don't know what those are—and you'll both end up feeling weird and low when the encounter doesn't work out as you'd hoped. People, whether they're aware of trauma or not, will still be receptive to wanting to make you feel good about what's happening. For most of the boning populace, knowing where to touch someone is a common part of getting down.

Hearing different people's versions of this leaves me more cognizant of future bedmates' feelings, which is very *party* for all involved. The mimesis of respect, as it spreads, helps us all improve collectively as serial, rampant pervs and devoted couples and clandestine oral-in-the-closet-after-work friends and those of us in good one-night standing until we all end up finding ourselves in a sexual golden age of consent. A girl can dream, right?

In the Act

Now that you are set up in terms of how and where to find a hot person and squire them to the nearest available love shack with both your health and inner ethical compass in tow, let's try not to blush over the specifics of *how* to establish yourself as a world-class fuck. While each sexual act, as discretely performed by each person, will not look or sound the same even as executed by the same partner later on, there's one absolute, all-enveloping way for all of us to rule at sex: *Never assume when you can ask instead.*

Following this protocol gives you the intelligence you need to find out what your partner likes most (and basically guarantees *consensual seduction*, to coin a phrase that I would rather abstain for the rest of my life than use aloud). Let's say someone neuron-splicingly enticing is going down on you. (Hello? It's impolite to leave someone hanging when they're trying to give you daps—hell yeah get it get it.) As this is happening, they look up at you, and ask, "Do you like it like that?" as if there were a mote of a chance you could refocus your eyes right now. But…you also like another kind of head gesture at which you think they'd excel. When you tell them, they're eager to prove you right.

Who knew this kind of orgasm was possible?!, she exclaimed over a hypothetical that doesn't have to stay one. Oh—normal normalsons who converse maturely and autonomously, instead of dunces operating under the self-congratulatory, self-concerned mindset that they are TOTALLY SLAMMIN' ROCK 'N'

ROLL SEX-HEROES WHO KNOW PRECISELY HOW TO *WORK THAT BOD*, aka those people who are usually excessively terrible in bed. Everyone's got their own specifications on what constitutes a rock 'n' roll sex-hero. (Mine is Debbie Harry of Blondie.)

It is stupidly easy to be the kind of person who *is*, or is in the process of becoming over time, a formidable lay. All you have to do is utter some close approximations of the question "Do you like it?" and sometimes add the word "how" in front of it. You can *very steamily interrogate* them beforehand and kill two birds with one bone: Sexual tension is my favorite way to get high (besides a couple of other ones). I recommend the entrance interview below for this, and because it helps you work toward the real-world application of its answers. It sets the precedent that they'll do the same for you, too. How does the adage go? Right: Lead by (devastatingly erotic) example.

If someone's response to "How do you like to be touched?" is the sincere, yet kinda-irksomely opaque classic that goes, "Whatever you do feels good," or if they're not down with announcing what they like out loud (and that's keen, too!), here are some devastatingly erotic examples of how to give the performance of a lifetime until you've supplied your own understanding of what that means for you two.

In the following suggested courses of action, you will not find the syllabi provided by women's magazines that ask you to lingually slip an ice cube or a hair tie over the penis of your poor, unsuspecting mark, or the misguided vaginal slapping that occurs with peculiar regularity in machismo-fogged pornos. Sorry and/or you're welcome.

The next part of this book establishes, instead, general tactics for performing a few run-of-the-mill acts, and variations on how to personalize sex. Try all of it. No matter what you're doing, do it like the entire meaning of life can be translated through your sexual talent...because, if you do, that's kind of true.

KISSING'S NOT DEAD

Kissing may seem so chaste, in the context of sex that involves more body parts than your lips alone. It's not. Being a good kisser is elemental to almost every other sexual undertaking, even if it's only because you know what's up when it comes to using pressure well. How you make out with one person might be totally different from how you french another, so it doesn't get boring as long as you're curious about that.

Kissing isn't just about your lips, anyway. Pay attention to where your hands go—to shoulders, the sides and/or back of necks (this area is flush with nerve endings, and it's nice to imagine them racing around under your fingers), hips, waists, and the smalls of backs.

Eyes-wise, some people are uneasy when the person they're frenching keeps the shutters open, but, as I have thought since first hearing this as a kid: How would you know if someone was both open-eyed and –mouthed unless you were? Those people are full of it!!! If they weren't, they literally wouldn't see the difference.

ORAL MYSTERIES

Squished somewhere between "breakfast lasagna" (regular lasagna eaten before 12 p.m.), Buffy Sainte-Marie, and the fact that "fostering kittens" is defined as *getting to hang with three tiny cat-cubs until they mature into sullen jerks*, oral sex occupies a top spot on the list of all that's worth spending time on. Giving blow jobs and eating pussy are my sexual pay dirt: I'm most turned on by other people's sexual pleasure, so my personal taste is that *tasting other persons*, a horrible euphemism for going down on people, has the highest value of any tendered sexual act. This doesn't have to be true in your case, but for me, it means not that I am expecting something in return, but it's usually the simplest way to knock off somebody's socks. (I ask you to reconsider your judgment if you are having sex with a person who hasn't already removed them.) Its recipient can't replicate what I'm doing by themselves, so if you shred at giving head, you become a specific kind of sexual asset. This goes doubly if you serve them a baked Italian pasta dish in the morning should they stay over.

I had to learn to love going down on people the not-always-good old-fashioned way: trial and error. There was *so* much error, in my early years: "watch your teeth" = the heavily reprised prayer flung at this halfway-feral teenage seraphim of the third base. The archaic practice of blindly hoping you're doing something right—of ascertaining whether that's the case *only* by interpreting moans—isn't as worthwhile when you realize that you can open your mouth for one of its other uses: talking about it.

HOW TO FINGER

Fingering someone can mean more than simply putting two digits inside the vagina in question. Some people love being stroked through their underwear, or their clits touched with just a finger or two, or having a person fuck them with part (or all) of their hand.

The feminine handjob can be its own pet—more than a stopgap during the approach to lingual or genital…jobs. If you're involved in sex of the latter case, fingering can efficaciously ready a person with a vagina for penetrative sex. So: You can shuffle fingering in with other acts, but it feels impeccable on its own.

Look at your partner's vagina—the positioning of her labia (outer lips), clitoris (small, circular, nerve-ending-packed area at the top of the orifice), vulva (inner lips), and so on. You can make someone's day without being able to define just what it is you're touching, but I find that degree of talent rare…and if you're a man who is totally 100 percent positive there's no need to bother knowing what the parts of a vagina are because you know intrinsically that you've got it all figured out, you are very likely wrong about yourself, I'm sorry to say. Knowing how to label an anatomical diagram is just the beginning of fingering someone. Here are some more stravagems:

There are preparatory concerns that shouldn't be overlooked. Rather than trying to cram a dry hand into your partner, make sure your fingers are wet. Put your fingers in your mouth or use some lube to make it feel natural instead of weird and arid. Why do some people think that pummeling you with their dry knuckles, as though you're scrapping in the street over some sports misunderstanding or something, is exactly what provokes orgasms? I want nothing to do with those kind of fisticuffs.

What's up with your nails? If they're long, don't put them on a very sensitive part of your partner. This is the vaginal equivalent of toothy head, so invest in some nail clippers and come back later. (But not too much later, please.)

The sensitivity of most clitorises is tough to adequately understand unless you have one yourself. You know how being tickled is pleasant enough if someone does it lightly, but almost hurts your insides when it feels like too much? It's like that, kind of, but even more intense. I like getting fingered most when people start outside of my panties. The subdued friction gets me acclimated and makes me want to rip the person's clothing to tatters with my teeth.

Underneath that: With two non-parched fingertips (you can also put them in your partner's mouth, if you're super hot) pass over your partner's clitoris quickly back and forth, skating on it carefully. If you've settled that they should talk about what they like, they'll tell you if they'd like to be handled with less fragility.

If you keep going, start by easing one finger inside unless you're directed differently. Slowly push your index finger in until it can't go farther, then remove it slowly and methodically, as though withdrawal were the entire point of this. Do that a few more times, quickening the time signature as you go. If you haven't yet, move to two fingers if you're being met with audible gratitude. Listen for what she likes, or have her tell you.

On the Spot

Every person touching a V can learn to locate a G-spot, which is found in a little area way inside a vagina, up against the top of it. It feels spongy and, for those who are having it touched, heady as fuck when gentle pressure is applied to it.

When your finger is all the way inside a person and the non-fingernail side is facing the ceiling, make the come-hither motion like a sleaze in a 1950s movie set in Europe twice in a row and, if you've found it, watch your partner bug out. For extra fun and entertainment, listen to them try and make conversation in full, grammatically accurate sentences for an hour after you finish.

HOW EAT PUSSY

It's 12:29 p.m.and I literally just cracked a domestic beer in satisfied preparation for this section. This is one of the most gloried aspects of all of time and space. I know I sound like a guru from southern California with this. I don't care! This is what I mean when I deflect a certain question by offering up that "I consider myself, you know, spiritual?" The oracular and mystic truth I can impart here: There are so many ways to be a god at this.

Stop time in the beginning. For the first few minutes you're giving head—and this whole act may last a very long while, which, in sex's altered time zone, sometimes means "upward of twenty minutes"—you'd do well to elongate every single one of your movements by going at about half the speed at which you're naturally inclined.

Mentally outline the parts of your partner's vagina by also

tracing them with your tongue. As you're taking your time, you can make a map key of their responses to being touched in each area. Go over again, and press with your lips and tongue more firmly, then softer, then harder, at alternating speeds and patterns of motion. Responses to these, both physical and spoken, will decipher how they like to be eaten out.

Outside of your tongue-cartography, less thorough strategies are worth exploring, too. Use your whole tongue, flattened out, like you would hold it out to accept a tongue depressor, but stationary and firm. Sharpen it to a point. Focus on flicking it across small individual areas, especially her clitoris. Touch the rest of the person's body with your hands, especially their breasts, and look at them, which will prove extremely useful when you're masturbating to this mental picture later.

You can and probably should fuck them with your tongue, taking occasional breaks to kiss their clitoris, although be sparing with that if they seem squirmy or overwhelmed—while some people love relentless, dedicated contact, others loathe to be tickled.

If you want to use your fingers while you also give someone oral sex, they'd probably love that. When you're using both your hands and mouth, it can feel like a lot to undertake at once. What, you are supposed to traverse this whole breathtaking (and neck-straining) landscape in a way that makes them moan like they're being paid for footage of it, while ALSO trying not to let how turned on you are by them distract you from the matter at mouth...AND finger-fucking them? If you'd like to try this but are anxious that it's all too balletic to do at once, use your fingers in a simple in-out motion and add movements as you go.

Be mindful of your nose. If you've got a honker, I am 57 percent likelier to find you very cute, but that statistic corresponds also to how much warier I'm going to be of your putting it near certain parts of me. When people dip their heads to pay attention to some lower region, they sometimes end up grazing with their noses, which can feel very nice...or very intense and weird, depending on how endowed the head-giver is (size does matter, in this respect) and how heavily they're breathing. Don't poke your schnozz where it doesn't belong.

HOW TO GIVE A HAND JOB

Place your non-dominant hand around the base of a penis, making a ring with your index finger and thumb. With your main hand, loosely make the "OK" symbol with your thumb and forefinger as you read this. That's the grip you want to use, just with your other three fingers closed, too. Tighten your hold gradually as you go, but avoid a manual stranglehold.

Shift your hand, and the firm-feeling subcutaneous part of your partner it's closed around (you will be able to tell the difference—skin/dick are in two utterly separate tactile zones on both ends of this act), down just a few centimeters. Hold your hand taut—although not TOTALLY immobile.

You don't want to dead-hand anybody, so, be very gentle as you alleviate the pressure you use here, then increase it again. As you massage the top more vigorously with your other hand, with very minimal gestures and movements, stroke and massage the base with that non-dominant hand every so often.

This might sound complicated, seeing as you'll have swifter actions in motion with your other hand, but...you can type, right? Do you understand how much more complex and involved that is, comprehension-wise, and yet, you do it by memory every day? Hand jobs are functionally simpler, and, instead of boring-ass emails about the time of tomorrow's meeting being rescheduled, you are making someone come.

With your dominant hand closed, slowly massage the length. Once you've gone up and down a few times, focus on the top for a minute, keeping the movement consistent, but a little gentler, and over a shortened distance, where the shaft meets the head.

The ultimate showstopping move is cake. Try another right-now demonstration: Hold the palm of your dominant hand out with your fingers open. Close your hand so your fingers meet your palm. Count to three as you drag your fingertips along your skin, up slowly to the ball of your hand, stopping at their bases. Imagine imitating that soft, rolling touch around a penis. Or just go do that to a penis, if you have one handy. (Stop looking at me like that. I know what I just said, and I apologize.)

HOW TO GIVE A BLOW JOB

Giving a blow job is far less laborious than that name for it implies, but that wasn't always as true for me in the past. Here's an approximated transcript of some long-ago trepidation on this front: *I'm supposed to give head? Do I do anything with my tongue? ARE TONGUES DISGUSTING? Ugh, this mouth-piece is like half sponge, half larvae...and it's a part of my anatomy? "Sorry, I have TMJ. It just happened just now. I think I caught it at the bank; they never sanitize those pens."*

Maybe you aren't exactly salivating at this idea for some similar reason, but I hope you are. I was missing out when I let primness stop me from deep-throating someone I was into. That's right: Believe in yourself and inhale that dick entire. Hold on a sec as I embroider this on a folksy/decorative sampler as a reminder to stay positive—good things can happen when you rise to life's challenges.

I would imagine self-confidence about giving this type of head is more accessible if you are also in possession of a penis and know how a mouth applied to that appendage feels stupendous and how it doesn't. It's still pretty basic, though. There are fairly trusty dicktates that can aid you in doing this well.

If you've watched porn that depicts a blow job, you could have all kinds of wild notions of what's expected of you and how to execute that, but at least one thing about BJs in skin pictures is true in reality: There is nothing hotter than someone looking up at you while you're getting head. Make eye contact for at least half of the time you've got a penis in your facial vicinity! (If this feels overly ambitious, shyness-wise: Your recipient's eyes may be closed for a lot of this anyhow.)

Looking up means that you've got some perspective about how someone is responding to each thing you do. It's also improving upon that, since it's slutty and porn-reminiscent, but doesn't look like a sham, and because it telepaths the hot transmission that this is about *them*. It opens both of you to enjoying it in your own interconnected, impossible-to-counterfeit mutual presence, whereas closing one's eyes feels more anonymous and avoidant of that. (However! If a person closes their eyes while they're getting head, it doesn't mean they don't want to look at you because what's happening isn't sufficiently hot—it's probably because it is, but they're trying to make it last longer by not staring at you.)

You can change the warmth, intensity, and friendliness of your expression to match the mood of the sex you're having. I like keeping my head tilted down, eyes fleeting up to meet the other person's. When my vision is met by the other person's, I nonverbally endeavor to say one of three things, or sometimes all of them in unison, from where our sight lines intersect:

1. *I can't believe I'm doing this and am having more fun than I knew was possible.* This face-place is a kind of innocuous, wide-eyed thing that has effects on any hunky simpleton—especially if they consider you an astoundingly proficient, authoritative person in areas beyond sex. But you are a precocious novice that they're teaching how to take a dick! You're so grateful to them! And so committed to doing the best possible job! HAAAAA. This is distinctly entertaining and slutty because of how separate it is from reality... otherwise known as how having imaginative sex works.

2. *You are so goddamn lucky.* Okay, imagine (or maybe recall) that this person had long been watching you, and wanting you, and barely daring to hope that you might someday be in

this position with them. They know you know that they tried not to look at you so obviously and did a terrible job at that. Imagine feeling that power over them, and then deciding, *You know what?* You're bored and they're cute—it'd be fun to grant them this...not that it means anything, as far as you're concerned, smirk smirk. I spontaneously looked up and winked at a dude I was kneeling in front of as I acted out this droll routine once, and though we're platonic bros now, he still brings it up as one of the sexiest things he's ever borne witness to. I have since made a practice of it.

3. *I'm going to get you harder than you've ever been, okay?* This one is direct and unabashed. Hold your eyes to theirs for as long as you can. Raise an eyebrow if it doesn't feel like too much of an affectation...says the person who just made an impassioned case for winking with a dick in your mouth, HAR! This is more declarative and sincere, though—and a lot louder and handsier, on your part (and so probably theirs too).

A few other things to consider:

• **Make sure your mouth isn't dry.** There's nothing more uncomfortable than trying to stuff a mouth that feels occluded with wool. Truly great blow jobs are palpably wet for both parties. You want to work up double the spit you're normally packing, and then veneer your partner's whole penis with your tongue. I keep a seltzer going while I'm giving head: Making noise, sucking, licking, and so forth have the tendency to dehydrate you with a quickness.

• **Pay attention to each part of your mouth's textures and capabilities.** You use your mouth for frenching, talking, and licking ice-cream cones/lollipops/other delectably phallic digestifs, if you live a life worth a damn. Adapting those movements to work with head can rule. Draw a line up from the base of a D with your tongue, softly kissing and breathing as you go. Press parts of the length of the dick into only the outermost areas of your lips.

Close…not your whole entire mouth, but most of it, on your partner's dick. Ease it back into your throat. Repeat. I mostly keep my teeth out of this arrangement by making my lips into a gentle barrier over them. Giving dome sans chompers might seem like a non-negotiable rule of head, but there are exceptions if you're fastidiously cautious: Some people like super-tender dental action if the majority of their penis is outside of a mouth. Don't chew with your mouth full (unless someone asks you to, which has never come close to happening to me).

• **Pretend you're starring in a stop-action blue movie.** When I was a blow-jobber on the make, I behaved like the body-double—or, I guess, head-double—of Ms. Pac-Man: I used to get so into how MUCH of a person's cock I could take into my mouth in the fastest possible sequence. Giving oral sex had become one of my favorite things, and since it was new to me, I was a bit over-eager. After some careful meditations on the responses I was getting from my partners and the ancient wisdoms foretold in video smut, I realized that it was probably worth trying out pacing myself. While Ms. Pac-Man is one of my style/life icons in so many ways—we have the same beauty mark and affinity for elegant hair bows and soft pretzels—she's not a good model for how to suck a dick. It's easy to slow down: How good a dick feels in your mouth often indicates that your mouth feels good to that dick. Acting on how the giving-of-head is nice *for you* is better for your partner, too.

• **Try using just your tongue for a moment.** Hold your partner's penis inside your mouth, curve your tongue around it, and use the tip to massage the base of your partner's dick. Slide the top of your tongue up along the center vein on the bottom of the penis as you go. The wide flatness of your tongue creates a pleasant suction and some of the filthiest sound effects known to your thread count. Don't bear down TOO hard with your tongue—it shouldn't feel like you're trying to PUSH the person's dick with it—or too wimpily. Laconically wind your tongue around the head—try clockwise, then reverse your circles, then back again.

Since this is the most sensitive area, the more you touch it, the more expeditious your partner's orgasm might be. If you're treating head as a precursor to penetrative sex, it'd serve you well to keep this in mind so that you can fuck for longer than about seven seconds.

• **Use hands to assist.** Whether you're running them along the length of a person's body, reaching up to touch their chest, or using them to apply light pressure or stroke their lower genitalia, like their testicles or perineum (the flat inch or two of skin between the front and back), don't forget that your hands can enliven sexual acts focused on another. If you prefer to concentrate on what you're doing with your mouth, gently hold their hip bones or place your palms on their waist and forget about them. To use them with super-low effort, press a knuckle against their perineum. This is an extra-delicate part of the body, so using your fingertips might mean leaving behind accidental scratch marks, which isn't the kind of tactile sensation we're after today. When it comes to testicles, you can very softly hold them with one or both hands as you go, and/or swap your hands with your tongue and lick very softly as you stroke the top of your partner's penis.

• **Deep-throating is optional (but advised).** You aren't obligated to do this (or ANYTHING ELSE, obvio)—just see what you're comfortable with, depending on how long the penis in question is. Inch as much of it is feasible into the back of your throat, then see if you want to go faster after your first few efforts. I like to have my partners thrust, too. If you feel you could be into it, try it out.

• **Be loud.** If you're suppressing noises, don't bother. Once upon a time, I had a boyfriend to whom I had been giving head for a few months before I thought to ask him, "Can I do anything to make this better for you?" This was when I was tentative about what I did during sex, so when he said, "It seems like you're afraid of being messy or making noise. I *like* it when I can hear you!" I was taken aback. I thought that preserving my neatness and decorum was paramount to seeming hot while fooling around. (It was nearly as surprising when this was further debunked to me earlier this year, when a different dude said, "Smeared makeup is sexy— it means you're really into it." Turns out what I thought read as "disheveled" was perceived as "erotic as heck." (I wish this were true in every last arena of life: "My closet is alluringly devil-may-care.") He was right: Good head can come with spitting, occasional gagging, and other sound effects. You can even audibly half hum, half moan while the whole, or majority, of a person's penis is in your mouth. Pass the noise through your tongue, letting it vibrate against your partner's skin, as you do what you normally would. The sound track you provide might come with less premeditation. Or you could always talk, one of my preferred ways of making noise during sex.

• **Spit? Swallow? Get it all over thine face?** What you do when a person is coming depends on your taste in both literal and figurative senses. *De gustibus non est disputatem*, and neither is how you choose to receive come. A secret: Lots of dudes privately love their own semen, as delivered mouth-to-mouth. There's always exploring that option!

Where to Position Yourself

Penetrative sex, whether you're having it vaginally or anally, can be approached from many different angles. You can be creative here without pretzeling yourself and your partner into an overly ambitious, tantric-ass tangle! It might sound boring, but I like positions that allow me to see as much of my person's body as possible—especially the ones I don't get to when they're clothed—which sometimes means missionary. Any way you can fit your body with your person's, or with a toy that they're using, is right as long as you like it. Try combinations of face-to-face, face-to-floor, face-against-a-mirror, *et alia*, of which you can conceive, and you'll know where to position yourself forever after.

AN INTRODUCTION TO ASS

Anal stimulation is in a class of its own, pleasure-wise, regardless of your gender or sexuality. It's up to you whether you find this "gross" or not, but I'm disinclined to write off something so matchlessly hot as "ew totally disgusting." You use every other appendage or orifice mentioned here for more than one function, and hands, if there were some argument to be made about which are least hygienic, take the cake. But I'm not the kind to raise those points in reality.

If you're freaked out by anything anal, please try to suspend your anxiety for a moment and consider the following: Taking something near or in your ass feels good like no other sexual contact—it's entirely its own brand of rad. The amount of next-day accolades I've received from a person who was trying anything anal-related for the first time could fill a modest trophy case with obscene-looking statuettes. The reward of easing into this bit by bit far outweighs the non-risk of feeling dirty. Look: I can't handle bathroom jokes because I find them excessive, and I love to eat ass.

If you're skittish for a more identity-based reason...why? I've encountered male partners who worried that it means that they are WAY GAY, or at least effeminate. I'm offended by both "concerns"—what's so horrific about being either, bro? However: I also understand that, from mondo-young ages, men are very often socialized to believe that either state, as doubled up with manhood, renders them unlovable, undesirable, and of lower worth than more traditionally masculine dudes. It's so dumb. To put this in terms with which people of other genders might be able to better empathize: You know how hyperaware women are that it's ruinously devaluing, or at least distracting, to buy the lie that you have to be two-dimensionally thin (except, of course, in your butt and chest zones), pretty, and otherwise SUPER-FEMME? You know how, sometimes, it doesn't matter how gravely you know that that's bull hockey—you just want someone to tell you you're beautiful, goddamnit??? Even the most well-intentioned men can go through similar mental capitulations—they know better than to assume "masculine" poses, but if they're observed making other kinds, it's hurtful, depending on who's looking. Gender norms brand you for life!!! They're so awesome that way.

If you're with a dude who is nervous on this front (or if you are one who's looking to tell a partner you want to try this), a helpful reminder is that men's bodies are anatomically designed to respond to prostrate stimulation. It has zero to do with gender-subversion unless you want it to (which is awesome, also, but maybe not the best immediate lead-in for anxious straight men who are just getting started in this arena). If the concern is that this means you have a manufacturer's error, sexually, for curiosity about more than straight-up vaginal penetration, please be bolstered by the reality that openness about sexual experiments of this and every ilk gives partners proof that you're a worthwhile fuck.

Outside of societal anxieties, the recipient may be worried about pain. I am sympathetic to this: If executed hastily, which is to say without lube or foreplay, or by receiving too much, too soon, anal penetration can definitely hurt. A lucky truth: Avoiding pain is so much easier than screwing up. All you have to do is get ready, which is hot in its own right.

Have your partner lie comfortably facedown on the bed. A from-the-back approach is the most intuitive at first. Spread their legs with your hands so that you can see. With your whole tongue, lick slowly up and down, then back and forth, and keep it light when you start so that it's kind of a tease and they find themselves wanting you to do more. Pretend you're giving highly concentrated head: Instead of a whole genital area, you've just got this one quarter-sized circumference to deal with. Ease your tongue in and see what happens. As you're touching them, be sure to also work some area of their body that you know makes them feel good in any other sexual configuration.

If you're inserting a finger (or anything else), make certain you've got plenty of lube close at hand (and all over your hands). Drench your person's orifice and whatever's going in it before penetrating them with a single finger. Rub your partner's asshole and slowly insert one. Lead with more fingers, then whatever else you have in mind. If you don't have a penis, you don't necessarily need a sex toy—it's up to you and your partner how much is enough. Whether you use a synthetic appendage or just your hands, pay attention to pain—your partner will help you. Start slow for the first few times, at least.

Let's (Not) Spend the Night Together

The main thing to keep in mind about choosing to spend the night at someone else's, or having them board at yours for the evening, is that it shouldn't connote any extra affection—*or* any lack thereof. If someone asks you to big-spoon them for the evening, it doesn't mean that they foresee your being part of the same place setting in the future. They might just be trying to be considerate, or angling for morning sex when you're both actually sober and at the height of your powers again, or maybe they just want to be ladle-cradled for a few hours. So don't go registering for a towel set embroidered with your two sets of initials in preparation for your imminent marriage after you split the next morning.

I am of the opposite school: In most cases, unless I DO want to date someone (and still even then), I am apt to split— or, if I'm at my place, say, "Can I walk you out? Do you need me to call you a car?" to the would-be spooner whom I'd rather have not occupy my bedspread. This is not always the case, but it is most of the time: I want to snooze by myself.

It doesn't mean I don't like them, or that I didn't have a great time. I find that sleeping next to someone, and then waking up all blearified the next morning and continuing to hang, is more intimate than I usually like to get with casual partners.

Seeing me naked is one thing—bodies are bodies, and mine hasn't altered that fact in either direction—but seeing me with my mascara smeared out to both of my temples, making jovial chatter at my favorite diner for reading or sharing an appetizer sampler among friends? WHOA, WHOA, WHOA, LET'S KEEP THIS LIGHT.

I'm an insomniac who worries over disturbing another person, but even if I am tired, I can be funny about the marital-feeling arrangement of snoozing side by side. I get all like, "DON'T YOU KNOW I PREFER ONION RINGS TO ENGAGEMENT ONES, YOU INTERLOPER? I did not know you murmured in your sleep, which is cute, but very intimate." I say it way more politely, and with plenty more omissions, than that.

My manners are unerring when it comes to all my partners, even the lackluster ones. Wanting to be considerate is *why* I ask them to leave—I don't want to end up resenting them for fulfilling what is maybe the very most basic and blameless human need after we involve ourselves in another less-essential but still-really-essential one.

There are extenuating considerations here, so a good rule of thumb if you're as hard-lined about these things as I tend to be: Try not to have sex with anyone you wouldn't also be amenable to waking up near, and don't have sex with someone in a place, physical or emotional, that would cause you to be hurt if you were asked to leave it.

I would MUCH rather that most of my paramours hit the road after we get together, but I compromise if it's egregiously late at night, if they're inebriated, if I can tell they'll feel totally uncomfortable or wounded if I ask them to scram (it's not that I'm advocating for placing someone's needs above your own ALL the time—it's just that, in this instance, I don't care *that* much), or if I anticipate the sunny-side-up sex with the good egg beside me will be just the thing. In those cases, they are free to come chomp fried foods at the diner with me come sunrise (well, more like high noon, if it's a weekend), despite all that that is bound

(continued)

to reveal about *the interiors of my deepest heart*. (I never said I was not a steadfast lunatic.)

If these concerns are not in play, I'm very delicate about how to withhold an extended invitation minus any perceived rancor toward my guest. Odds are, I had a lovely time and would be mortified to communicate anything to the contrary. When I have cause to believe someone might take my real feelings poorly, I pull out a true excuse.

I have a job that requires twelve-hour days of me, many of which I log at home while the rest of the world sleeps next to their sexual partners peacefully. I can guilelessly plead work obligations, a lot of the time. If you're having sex with me, you very likely already have come to know how heartily I prioritize working—*even more than sex, if you can believe it*—and expect this outcome.

In some situations, I've had to use suaver language to give people the slip. I do this mostly by being honest, but if this sounds convincing enough to work for you, I exhort you to swipe my technique. Try to save it for a bit longer than the precise moment after climax, though, for kindness's sake: "I'm so glad you/I came over—hanging out with you rules and I like you a lot. [IMPORTANT NOTE: Say that very last part only if it's true.] I have lots of work I've got to get done by first thing in the morning. I don't want you to feel rushed or uncomfortable, so I think it's probably best if we call it here, while I'm still mobile and halfway presentable." If you want to see them again, end by saying when.

It's best to get your intentions re: the length of any visit cleared up prior to arrival, whether you're the host or the guest. If I am visiting someone, I like to say, "Can I come over for a few hours before I have to go back to work/before my big day tomorrow?" or, if a person's coming around mine, "Want to stop by for [INSERT JUST-UNDER-MAXIMUM AMOUNT OF HOURS I CAN ALLOT FOR SEXUAL MAYHEM HERE] before I've got to get ready for tomorrow/to go do [INSERT NON-SEXUAL-MAYHEM ACTIVITY HERE]?" That way, no one's feelings are at risk of being surprise-attacked by my very attractively aloof and freakadocious schedule/need for privacy.

If you prefer that someone spend the night, or that you monopolize their zone for the evening, say that outright! "Do you want to sleep here?" or, "Can I come over tonight and stay with you?" are just as sexy as less time-specific invitations—and less confusing. If your bedmate has the same poise that you do, they will say yes and then make good on that promise, or do like me and say, "I can't stay over, but I can come by," and then you are free to make whatever decision you need to based on that updated timeframe.

SWEET EVERYTHINGS

Do you want to talk some good filth, but remain perhaps too nervous? Clear your throat and read this lexicon of non-wince-inducing things to say mid-liaison, complete with instructive ideas about when to dispatch each of them! Note: The following passage does not include the phrases "flesh bundle," "yonic wizard," or any of Jim Carrey's "hit" catchphrases from either of the blockbuster hit franchises *The Mask* or *Ace Ventura*, aka the erotic lexicon I was very tempted to pass off as "smutsational" in this passage. Somebody stopped me...and that "somebody" was my own danged moral conscience. Fine! Or should I say...*all righty, then...*

Articulating yourself with respect to filth is a gratifying undertaking. You'll find you achieve better returns, sex-wise, if you hone the terms you use to speak about fucking, both in anticipation of it and during. That dialogue is at its very best when a person has mastered their personal smut-vocabulary, which is to say, exclamations more specific than, "I love it when you do that... thing...that's happening!" If you're not yet confident in your own dirty mouth, I have plenty to say.

When I say *personal vocabularies*: Learning how to talk dirty from porn is like learning to speak French without any immersive instruction. Porn will give you a basic idea to work from, just like with blow jobs, but if you don't expand on that yourself through interactions with actual people, your directives end up sounding like prerecorded customer service lines, and not even sex-centric ones. Since we're not *quite* at the point in the future where we solely fuck robots, let's enjoy human interfacin' as best we know how, which is sometimes…flawed or unwieldy, pride-wise. That does not have to be the case each and every time, though—press "2" for more options, or let your fingers continue to do the walking via continuing to turn these pages.

Talking about fucking is equally as hot when you're not simultaneously living out the events you're narrating. Some of my favorite filthy conversations have taken place over text, chat services, the phone, and long letters. The beauty of letting others overhear your dirty mouth before you're together physically is framing yourself as v. buckwild without yet having to prove it, which is great if you're titchy with new partners, which I can be sometimes.

No matter how you conduct yourself in bed, sex-based correspondence allows you the freedom to dictate how that is perceived. The suggestion of you, and all the things you want to do, has the benefit of padding a memory/expectation of the way you have sex with the other person's fantasy, as ghostwritten by you. You can make provocative revisions to your entry in another person's sexual biography by annotating it before or after the fact of your introduction into the record.

The sexiest conversations I've ever had were thanks to people with the knack for getting me off on statements that could sound weird coming from someone else, but are perfectly natural as uttered by the person saying them. Compare two different occasions on which I deliquesced in my chair upon receiving these incontestably dissimilar raunch-missives:

- "I don't really have the time or focus to write you a proper letter, but I feel like I should send you a note because it would be almost dishonest not to, since you've been in my mind so often today, and have generally improved my disposition, apart from whatever I might have been specifically thinking about you. It would be enough to me to keep my affections for you alive, since after all they are more or less unlimited. Still, I think of studying your pussy with the respect and mineral hard-on it's due." (—An email, or "filthy mash note," as he called it, by an august writer I dated for a few months)

• "ugh. i wannnnna lick your ass before the super bowwllll" (—A gchat from a sports-obsessed bro with a great dick with whom I was sleeping for a moment and a half, around the same time as I was seeing Mineral Hard-On)

Both of the wishes expressed above were honored. They straightforwardly got me thinking about each of these partners' merits, respectively, and I couldn't wait to continue the discourse in person. I recognize the places in which these notes are corny, and that makes me even *more* into them! Everyone is corny, and I am most willing to be undressed by people who don't let that stop them from perving out on/with/in me.

How you phrase your own FILTHY MASH NOTES is up to you, but here's a helpful script: While "What are you wearing?" serves as a time-honored workhorse of an introduction, I typically lead by talking about what part of a person's body my brain is obsessively posing in compromising positions, or by dissecting my most longed-for ideas about what I want to do together.

The other day, a somewhat mild person with whom I'm sleeping offered his philosophy on compelling coital conversation. "It's always good to just say what's happening, or what you want to happen." He's right! When all else fails, imitate a horny David Attenborough and state exactly what's happening. (Draw the line, however, at imitating his accent.) In your fantasies, are you getting phenomenal head? Talk about what, exactly, they would be doing that'd make it feel so good. Are you bent over, or bending someone over, a couch with your clothes still on? Describe, in close detail, the extent to which you find that urgency sexy. Name specific body parts as smuttily as you can while still being earnest—"vagina" and "penis," though more than welcome physically, are words best saved for your doctor. Even if someone in the room is wearing a slutty nurse uniform, be less anatomically correct. (Unless you have been specifically asked to do otherwise, in which case, go ahead and speak clinically, ya amateur Dr. Love.)

Here is a pre-assembled sentence that even the most skittish amateur Attenboroughs can employ with ease, whether you're saying it in person or in writing: "I love it when you _____." Fill in the blank with the act in as much detail as you can: "I love it when you try to fit my cock all the way into the back of your throat." "I love it when you pull my hair while you're pinning me to the bed." *Et alia!* Add adjectives at will.

In EVERY guide to being a socialized person interacting with others within the labyrinthine confines of "speaking articulately and like a cool-type normal," there's one core tenet: When you're unsure what to say, pay a genuine compliment to your fellow conversationalist. You're having sex with this person for a reason, right? You decided you found their voice sonorous, or their wrists are so perfectly formed that you're ITCHING to kiss them in their fine entirety, or they have a truly flawless butt-shape. You can and should expound on those observations.

Whenever my co-bed-denizens have made me feel like I am the one person they're most excited to be fucking in that moment, and *exactly me only, that's it,* I put roughly 600 times more vigor into putting them into a blackout orgasm fog for the next few hours. How they've communicated this to me is by picking up on—and venerating—the peculiarities of the one body I'll ever own.

I see a lump of unleavened pizza dough in fake eyelashes staring at me from inside the mirror, so it was cool when one girl brought up my "beautiful cheekbones" (not a thing) when we were involved in a heated makeout. It also led me to notice what it was, exactly, that I found pointedly gorgeous about her, which were the freckles on her chest. In the easiest segue of all time, we both took our shirts off.

Your own encomiums don't have to hinge on a person's appearance (cf. that sexy vocal register), or any other of their empirical features, for that matter. I don't usually select potential sex partners based on how they look because I am a morally flawless person. (It's because I have face blindness, meaning that it's hard for me to discern the whole picture of someone's appearance even if I know them—rather than poor self-image, that's the deal with the pizza-dough dysphoria I mentioned above, also.) When I let someone know that I think they're the mad note, I focus on how to translate that opinion into something that might turn them on to hear about, which is interesting to do with non-aesthetic qualities.

All told, the crasser you can be, the better, but if you're taciturn or easily embarrassed by nature, it can feel simpler to say, "Touch me like that," or, "Put your mouth there," or "Hold my wrists down." That dialogue wouldn't even be censored on television. You're basically not even talking about sex, you chasteoid! Except you are, and it's soooooo hot, and your partner is thinking about/looking at you like TWO cartoon roast chickens on a desert island instead of just one.

Romantic Attachments

Sending links to porn, if a person has indicated that they like to watch it and would be down to do so with you, establishes you as a great listener *and* a hot fuck. Since many full-length porn videos are drawn-out productions in which we are treated to long, staredown-laden striptease intros during which viewers are asked to make note of an underwear company the actors are shilling for called something akin to "www.skinclothezzz.xxx.com,"

(continued)

I find it preferable, and more direct, to link to .GIFs *in medias res.* Think any activity that could be described by the word "guzzling," or whatever filthy analogue you're indicating that you'd like to imitate with the recipient. Five seconds is all you need to get your point across.

BLUE MOVIES

I have a running page in every journal I keep where I take note of a specific phenomenon whenever I notice it crop up. The "Equal Parts Love and Hate List" comprises all the elements of this life that can provoke an equilibrium of repulsion and enthusiasm in me, depending on my mood and the context in which it's getting under my skin (for better or for worse). The top entries on these lists:

• Frozen yogurt (love: delicious, creamy, low-cal, toppings; hate: the clear demarcation of a neighborhood being swallowed and prevailed over by a ruling upper class)

• Male attention (love: noticing subtle glances and thinking, *Why, hello and thank you, sir*; hate: being noticed by a stranger who is then compelled to scream at me about the right and wrong ways in which my body is shaped)

• Hanging out with small children for extended periods of time (love: *You are so canny, all discovering the world and comparing it to the scant other parts of the world you know about so far and making me laugh a lot*; hate: *You are so loud, plus definitely a barometer for whether I'm a good person or not based on whether you like me, and I don't want to know the answer to that*)

• The word "cleave" (love: it starts with a voiceless velar stop, which is the term for a hard "k" sound, my favorite; hate: anytime "cleave" is used biblically or sexually, ew)

• Reading about feminism on the internet (love: attention is being paid to inequality, and that like-minded people are globally able to rally around and converse about that; hate: when women dog or exclude one another for not allowing for female viewpoints that disagree with or come from a different experience than theirs)

• Country music (love: heart pangs and alcohol; hate: racism disguised as "down-home culture")

• Pornography, which I have quite obviously been waffling on addressing for this whole chapter thus far. Pornography is unusual because it's a silent partner in so many aspects of our lives: It's all around us, influencing so much of our intake and output of how we behave in ways both overt and covert. I'd rather do just about anything, including getting catcalled by randos, than talk unflinchingly and straightforwardly about the kinds of porn I watch. The prospect alone falls exclusively on the "hate" list. Parsing why this is not the case for the pornographic medium itself is tougher.

I am going to do my best to peer at the tension between liking and getting off to pornography and abhorring it with my whole self, because I think plenty of people share a similar discomfort with it. The main consideration as to when the last item hews "love" rather than "great pulsating hatred" in me: Am I watching a kind of porn I like and not confusing its plot devices with real-deal in-person cleaving (ugh), or am I in the wilds of the internet that can make me feel inadequate, grossed out, or that I am *not tan, thin, young, 'n' pube-shorn enough to ever be a candidate for sex again???*

Whether you love or hate porno (or both, or neither), it's up to you to dictate how you consume it. I'm not talking about *abstaining from jacking off more than once a fortnight, unless a southerly tide spells your name in seashells, the moon is a waning crescent, and no one else is home*, or whatever arbitrary time constraint has been culturally, internally, or interpersonally assigned to you as "right." What makes for healthy porn consumption is the answer to this question (which is contingent upon each individual person's comfort): Is taking in pornography fucking up your life in any tangible way you're actively aware of? Pornography addiction is a real condition, but unless you find yourself helpless against prioritizing porn to the detriment of unrelated areas of your life, like being unable to have sex with a partner without it if that hurts their feelings, it's unlikely that you have it. If you're unsure, ask a psychologist.

I love porn when it helps me alleviate sexual frustration or engage with a fantasy that I am either uncomfortable with or unable to share with any of the sexual partners I've got going at the moment. If I rely on it for my main interactions with sex and masturbation, I find myself looking for new extremes in terms of how out there it can be, which impedes my sex life because I feel dull for having uncomplicated sex, which I also usually love. Porn can be a resource, but it shouldn't be your only sexual point of reference.

I was also, for a long period, unnerved by pornography because I thought I was competing with it. It was like I was looking at a still life of some apples and being all, "DANG, guess I'm never eating real fruit again, now that I've seen that painted produce can do THAT; guess I don't have the right…seeds…" What I was forgetting: Porn does not have hands, a mouth, and so forth—most notably, it lacks actual consciousness, so it's ridiculous to envy it. I'd rather pay attention to how I can make the sex I have, be that by myself or with someone else, feel unique and right without the specter of some remembered camgirl looming over it.

There's no need to feel as though I have to live up to porn when I think about what draws me to it in the most basic senses. I watch porn whose actors frequently look nothing like my partners because I am happy with what my partners are all about and would like to see thoroughly contrapuntal acts and bodies that aren't already a part of my sex life. I also watch it, generally, because it gives me inspiration for things I can do with the people I have sex with.

Even if people in your life treat porn like an immoral cesspool in which sinners are drowning their deficient souls, it's more of a sizzlin' cabana party, from what I've seen on my computer screen. Much like a coconut rum–infused fuck-a-thon, it's pretty unbeatable in moderation: a nice diversion from real life, but not what you expect it to be like around-the-clock.

THE ETHICAL SMUT

Taking in a rude motion picture is the same as any other consumer choice—you can decide how to do it ethically. If you're concerned that the pornography you like to watch is disadvantageous to either the individual actors in it or our *twisted society-culture on the whole, man,* let's talk about how to make sure you're watching videos that you don't feel go against your moral code.

Are you mad at what you like because it doesn't square with your personal gender, race, class, or sexual orientation–based politics? I try to take a look at the way I conduct myself in the world, and reexamine what my *actual feelings and behaviors* about social justice, equal rights, and respecting people of all stripes are. *Yeah, yeah—they're pristine.* Except they're not, of course! Few people can be convinced of their bigotry, even when it's obvious that we live in a white supremacist patriarchy that imbues us with it. Look, I get that you're not currently guffawing heartily at a homeless person on your office flat-screen TV and smacking your secretary's ass while clad in a KKK uniform. However: If you were born white, male, straight, or cisgender, you were given a book of get-out-of-jail-free cards that was withheld from others, and if you're not trying to redistribute them in *all* things, including pornography, that's kind of a boner-killer for the rest of us.

In your broader life, do you make a concerted effort to lift up and listen to others in order not to bulldoze them? Great! Let's take a look at how that extends to your skinematic taste. Are you able to recognize, if you're watching porn that isn't a perfect representation of your politics (aka, 97 percent of porn), what and where the flaws are? Okay, then go ahead and watch it if you want to.

In many cases, in getting off to polemically tricky porno, it seems like people are exorcising its presence in the life they know outside their internet browsers—as a form of relief. I like some porn that is rough or intentionally derogatory toward women, just as I do sex that plays similar power games. If I ever experienced anything like the plots listed by my search history, or of previously agreed-upon and mutually respectful rough sex, when I hadn't agreed to it, the experience would be horrifying/traumatic. By taking pleasure in porn that embraces the horror-trauma plots that others might foist upon me and/or people with bodies like mine, I feel like I'm in control of and subverting the rape-culture-borne reality that I am a target. That's sexy to me. Porn can be a depressurized expression of all that is ridiculous and wrong in reality—a safe place to exercise sexual inclinations that you would shudder, panic, and feel hatred toward should they show up in earnest in your true-blue bedroom or life.

Shame, fear, displeasure, and anger, unlikely as it may or should seem, can interweave into the network of what a person finds desirable. This is not to say that those who like offbeat sex are damaged or flawed—finding a private, self-directed way to morph those feelings into something that feels good and self-determined means you are the opposite, because it's incredibly healthy. When you choose to let the nightmarish cartoon of hard porn play out before your eyes and you're able to feel pleasure and power instead of pain from making it your entertainment, you claim victory over it.

I have limitations within this. I would never be able to get off to porn if I were aware that the actors in it were being disenfranchised or forced or otherwise hurt by what they were doing. The majority of porn actors in "produced" porn movies, aka those videos that look like they were shot on a tripod and not the Droid of some guy named Mike, have willfully signed contracts to appear in their star vehicles. I love an autonomous adult-film impresario. Find actors who seem to take genuine joy in what they do.

Outside of that directive: Porn comes in all different categorizatons and search-bar terminologies. What you're looking for can be surmised from what you otherwise fantasize about when you masturbate. Distill it into one to three words, turn on private browsing, and go find it. I promise you that it is there.

I always worry that the videos I find on more generic porno search engines and amateur sites were leaked out of retribution without one of the parties' knowledge. I like to stick to "sex-positive" porn sites, even though, as I mentioned upfront, I feel word-negative about the hippie-dippie hey-man-it's-the-'90s-ish designation of that term. For amateur porn heads of my same ilk, here is the best way to find it: A few years back, the entrepreneur Cindy Gallop masterminded a blissful website called Make-LoveNotPorn. It collates the "Mike's Droid" style of cinematography, except the encounters are blemished, realistic, and taken by their own willing, loving actors (including couples, friends, one-offs, and more). Everyone in the videos is stoked to participate.

Think doubly hard about whether that's the case for the porn actors in videos of people who, identity-wise, maybe have a harder time with sex work. (This is a fraught topic; I'm scared that by advocating for a reduction in demand for income these people have is also a detriment to them.) People in the sex industry, especially marginalized ones, deserve support, your agitating politically and spreading the word for their protection, and pragmatic and social resources in areas that extend beyond your laptop. If a person is willing to get off to the employees of a field that cannot yet legally provide sufficient working conditions for all of those involved in it, then that same person turns off their computer and scoffs at or blithely rebukes these people, that person is a jerk-off in EVERY sense of the word. Do not let your reluctance to seem like a free-spirited tree-nerd override and inhibit your ethical decency, will ya? After all, man, it's the '90s. We know better these days.

GRAPHIC PHOTO-REALISM

Failing the whole internet: Make *your own* porn, whether you're doing so by means of still or moving images! Just smile for the camera, please, as we consider how to create fine works of art in both mediums.

Taking skin photos is likely going to involve some self-scrutiny regardless of whether you're trying to embody the very portrait of aesthetic grace or simply be arranged into a passably fuckable assortment of pixels. Don't beat yourself up if you spend an hour agonizing over the perfect lighting and angles, but please know you can also take a blurry shot of your butt that will be attractive in its own right. Do what feels good. When in doubt, take your picture from slightly above you in order to fit more of you in it (as seen from a universally flattering viewpoint!), make sure your posture is long and strong, and see if you can muster a smile if your face is in the frame.

When it comes to photos that include your whole torso, some people I know swear by the "S Curve," which some of my pals say they copped from the proto-edgy soft-porn site Suicide Girls, but which originated with the artist William Hogarth in 1753. It's universally venerated! The "line of beauty," as it's known most democratically among camgirls and eighteenth-century artists alike, is the shape of the letter its other nickname represents. What you do, to get that scurve on: Stand stationary. Choose a shoulder. If you favor your right, cock and shove it in the direction of the wall behind you. Tilt your neck heavenward toward your left shoulder—imagine you are uncoiling springs in it that allow it to stretch languidly. Point the nexus of your jawline and the side of your face on that same left side high-up, too, and push your left shoulder and hip in front of the rest of your entire self. Take a sip of something. Okay. Back to it: Align the right butt cheek/hip region with your right shoulder as far opposite the left side of your body as it will go. Sip. Snap the picture.

Or you could always do like me, say fuck it, and *cover your-self in value-menu cheeseburgers in the heart-shaped hot tub of a New Jersey love motel.* (See photo, below).

Credit: Nate "Igor" Smith

This photo is titled, "Twenty-two years of age, thrilled with herself, and makin' some choices."

If your face is a central part of your picture, either point your chin into your chest and fire your eyes directly at the lens, or float it toward the ceiling and do a heavy-lidded "god DAMN can you believe that you aren't here making love to my body?" face. Or cross your eyes and squeeze your chest together real hard and rest complacently in the knowledge that you are a hilarious person (all genders).

The most pressing part of deciding how to include thine vis-age in your photo: Imagine whether you'd be straight with it being seen by everyone you know—Your siblings. Your elemen-tary school teachers. Your colleagues. That probably—almost definitely—will not happen, but what if it did? Would you keep your S-curve intact as you strutted forth into the world, or would you feel more resolutely that your life was OVER? KAPUT? OH MY GOD, I NEVER WANT THEM TO SEE MY MOUTH IN PERSON AGAIN, LEST THEY RECALL ITS SENSUOUS PURSED-LIPNESS.

If you are in a position where you'd like to be extra-cautious with your photos, not because you are *afraid of sex*, but because you'd rather keep them private: Sorry, but consider not taking them, because there's no such thing as totally secure data anymore, even if the other person guards your attachments as closely as they can.

Before you lower your camera/phone/computer and put your pants back on: You've got other options. When I was first arranging myself into sultry-ish poses intended for the consumption of others, I never included my face, deciding instead to focus on body parts without clearly identifiable birthmarks on them (because I thought that people would recognize the Cindy Crawford blotch on my right ass cheek, having never seen it? I don't know) and sent them from a dummy email address registered to "Simone de Beauvoir." When I felt less skittish, I gradually showed more until I was totally cool with full-frontal (and back-al).

These days, I don't think I'd mind too terribly if "explicit" photos of me emerged for the consideration of the general viewing public, no matter if I weren't artfully censored by burgers. To my knowledge, there's no easy way to access my full-bore naked photos unless I want you to, though I think the number of people to whom I've sent explicit camera-phone selections nearly qualifies as "public," so I'm not very stressed out about it. People have seen human bodies that are more beautiful than mine, yes? Yes. People are aware that we are not brains floating around in white dress shirts clamped closed with buttons at the throat and wrist, paired with three-ply khaki snow pants with reinforced iron crotches, yes? I strongly hope, yes.

Some people are fearful that being sexualized, or sexualizing themselves, diminishes them in the eyes of others, especially professionally. I have had friends for whom this anxiety has been well-founded thanks to others' actions, if not reasonable or empathetic logic: A teacher pal was once disbarred from an enviable title after an anonymous person sent the administration for which she worked old-fashioned editorials of her from one of those too-expensive Euro magazines you can get only at the bookstore.

My friend protested her dismissal so cogently and persuasively that she was reinstated, with her students none the wiser, and I'm pretty sure that in five years it won't even fuck with your chances of running for Congress, if it even does now. Your life is never "over" if photographic evidence of your involvement in adult practices is discovered. The only trick is not acquiescing to shame. Shame wrecks your pride both sexually and to a larger, life-minimizing size. If my friend had rolled over (in a different sense than what was depicted in her contentious photo, I mean), she would be out of that job, and, worse, she would have been disavowing something she believes—*this is a hot thing to do, and who cares?* Shame doesn't make the situation go away. It makes you look pathetic, and you're not, so why act like you believe otherwise?

HOME FOOTAGE

Let's say you are well aware of the risks involved with DIY video smut. Your concern is not with security, but with quality: How do I shoot porno in the first place?

Here are some options:

• Use a camcorder. This seems laughably quaint—*hey! why not just go the extra mile and make one of those classic peephole flip-books of your butt-nudes?*—but if you want to make a private, one-edition-only memento (and what feels more lurid than secreted-away analog porno? You have to find a HIDING PLACE for it, just the thought of which is devastating me with hotness), dig the VCR and camcorder out of storage, or cop them for a dollar each at just about any yard or sidewalk sale, then take turns maneuvering the camera's point of view back and forth with your person.

• If you're using a phone: Handheld cameras are some of my favorite sex toys, and their perspectives and angles, as seen after they're recorded, are the most reminiscent of what fucking is actually like.

• If you're more likely to be distracted or made self-conscious by a camera all blatantly up in your face, set up a computer on a surface above the one where you'll be having sex. Keeping it on the bed with you *can* work, but a relaxed attitude toward the positioning can also leave you with a work of film like one that an old boyfriend and I made. The best part of making porn is watching it right after, and as we reviewed that one, we saw our sex lives as we never had before: The laptop had shifted around alongside our bodies, eventually settling on a tight shot of our two stomachs clapping against one another. It wasn't quite the movie we had intended to auteur, but it was a better comedy than most of what you'd pay to see in a theater, based on how hard it made us laugh.

ON FETISHES

Fetishes are another avenue for experiences you typically do not have and identifying new selves as you go along with the kinky shit at hand.

For a solid hunk of last year, I had sex with Jaskov, a brilliant rapper. I discovered that the only time he ever seemed withdrawn while talking to me—he was a world-class yammerer—was when, after we'd been boning for a fortnight, we started talking about whether we had any offbeat sexual proclivities.

"I have this…one thing," he admitted, sitting on top of my desk at 5 a.m. (my personal fetish: fellow nocturnes). He was so reluctant to vocalize his secret outright that he had me guess it. I tried in earnest for a while, but quickly cycled through the exceedingly common BDSM and gender-flipping stuff to no avail.

I would have to think harder. "Is it dungeons, but Dungeons and Dragons themed? No? Ben wa balls embossed with the faces of our founding fathers? Nah? Fine—it's drag, but we're wearing our normal clothes and SAYING we're in drag? Toe parties? What's a toe party, if yes? Are you attracted to snowpeople? I could put a carrot on my nose if you were into that. *Jas-kovvvv!* Are you into girls sitting cross-legged on super-burritos and wriggling their eyebrows lasciviously à la Groucho???!!!" I would have been down for all of this. (Especially the last one, as long as we ordered another for me as compensation.)

He pointed to my nose.

"Nostrils?" I said uncomprehendingly.

"Kind of. I like watching girls sneeze." He looked terrified by this admission.

I laughed, but not because this was worthy of mockery: I was *delighted*—and avid to begin. In college I could *absolutely* sneeze! I was the insufferable snuffler in every lecture hall scoring standardized tests with my six-part gasping and honking fits! (I get that I have now alienated every other sexual prospect I may have had outside of our boy Jaskov.) My dreadful sinuses were, in fact, an asset to somebody?!

"Dude! I am like the Big, Bad Wolf if he had allergies instead of legendary lung capacity," I said.

He stared. "Yes... I've noticed."

I considered this surreptitious style of pervin': "That must be both a convenient AND an inconvenient turn-on: I never thought about it before, but girls are sneezing everywhere."

"Yeah, like, you know how germy the subway is? I think I'm the only person alive whose favor that works in—except I try not to gawk, since it's impolite, and because they feel like it's because I think they're doing something gross when I'm the one who's guilty on that front." (He is a good, if peculiar, dude.)

I wondered what other boners I might have unwittingly

launched by guilelessly hanging out in the world—are people into untied shoes? (Is THAT what a toe party is?) Nail-biting? Smoking? Lipstick on front teeth? (I googled it, and the answer is yes on all counts. Take that, *gracefulness*: Turns out I'm perfect at sex after all!)

That night/morning, Jaskov taught me how to twist up snatches of tissues into soft, pointed utensils that induced loud outbursts when I prodded at my nose with them. Privately, I thought this was hilarious, this employment of tissues to aid and abet sneezes rather than deal with their aftermath. How beautifully backward.

I'd sit in my bed in low-cut T-shirts, pouting and feigning "a really bad cold coming on," and then pester my sinuses with a paper wand. Jaskov watched me, mesmerized by the preemptive, sharp sighs inward, then absolutely lost his mind when I had to sneeze. It was a colossal amount of fun. So, too, was watching his jaw drop, as promised, on public transportation the few times we left the house together. I knew that when he said, "God bless you," to me, he truly meant it.

Okay. I realize I have just relayed a strange tale of having sex with someone who got off on weak immune systems. But we had a great time, and since I liked making him come, it wound up turning me on, too. Isn't that wild? Sharing a fetish with a partner is a mad generous act on the part of their owners.

Only total jerk-offs, who deserve only to jerk off, meet "confessions" of Jaskov's kind with derision instead of gratitude. Even if you're not inclined to test-drive their proclivities, isn't it cool that they trust, respect, and find you sexy enough to let you know about it, even if "it" *is* callipygian honeys taking a seat on Tex-Mex delicacies?

It's so easy to feel shy. No one wants to seem like a WEIRDO, especially when it comes to their sexual fitness. That self-containment impulse is what keeps people from better-than-just-adequate physical coupledom. Here's a tiny primer on how to introduce your *shameful sexual horror-show behavior* (calm down; it's not; I'm fucking with you) to someone you're all sexed out about. And what to say (and abstain from saying) if someone is admirable enough to entrust you with theirs—that is, as long as they do it with your feelings in mind. Something uplifting to keep in your distorted mind (again: this is not a real thing) as you read: You know who definitely has at least 764 unique fetishes? Prince. I would go to a toe party of *his* any day of the week, no question.

If you are a freaq with a *sensuous secret*, you might wonder how to impart this information to your intended without humiliating yourself and/or discomfiting them. Ostensibly, you're breaking out your fetish with someone you trust enough to sleep with. That's a start! You can totally have individuated oddball sex straight out of the gate, but it's easier for me to work up to the really buck activities I fantasize about, no matter how SEX-POSITIVE (barf!) I and a partner may express to each other that we are.

I consider, too, that more casual flings, as far as they know, volunteered themselves for straightforward sex. While there's a chance that they'd be down to try other things, there's no guarantee they wouldn't feel cornered by my asking for them. I prefer to steadily hint my way in the door by testing out the tamest aspects of my fetishes. When I'm ready, I then say, "You know how we sometimes do [X THING] when we're fucking? I like that a lot, and I'm wondering if you'd be into doing more—like [X OTHER THING]."

As a consummate layabout (one of my many bona fides in this capacity: I am typing this to you facedown on an N'SYNC blanket with mysterious hot sauce stains giving Justin inflamed-looking psoriasis), I'm super amenable to fetishes that handily take a looming task off my Sriracha-laden plate. I was once in a relationship with a man who liked to depilate me. Joe explained his hobbyist aesthetician career thusly: "I'm obsessed with vaginas because they're so beautiful, so I like to see them as closely as I can. Tending to them makes me feel like I'm at the service of the thing I love most in the world." I was like, *Oh, word? Hold on while I grab the shaving cream for you real quick, because I hate doing it myself!*

We're adults, you know? The whole point of being an adult is discovering the weirdnesses of others with love instead of fear. There are so many favorite fixations of regular, hot people: humiliation, forced orgasms, voyeurism and exhibitionism, feet, and choking/erotic asphyxiation. And those are all pretty basic!

THREE EXTRA-SPECIAL FETISHISTIC FIREBRANDS

• **Gender-tangling.** One of my favorite gambits with male partners who are down is that they're my girlfriend—and this doesn't apply to all the dudes I've been with; just the handful of ones who've gregariously indicated they like it. It's always the most traditionally masculine guys who like this, I think because it's such a reversal of what they're expected or think they're allowed to do in reality, which always makes for sex. I tell them I'm going to give them head like I would to a girl—and I do it. Usually, gender-flipping is as much about the sexualized "shame" that guys are supposed to feel about being feminine or what have you; so, if they're into it, comment and capitalize on that as you go.

• **Rape.** This fetish isn't specific to one gender, or even to one idea of which gender is the attacker and which is the target. I like to tell dudes what they have to do as much as I like to "accidentally" leave the front door of my apartment unlocked and have them come up behind me as I'm working and stop me from it. It takes all kinds—and it's all totally fine. I'm always confused by men who dismiss rape fantasies as having to do with the meaningless catchall misogyny-net known as "daddy issues," since this is about, for me, taking a harmful, potentially mortal situation that

I have to be wary of and protected against in my day-to-day all the time, then defanging it and making it into a farce of which I am in control. What's *damaged* about making lemonade when life hands you rape culture? People who try to shame women for wanting to flip the script about one of the toughest parts of their daily realities should reconsider their positions. And leave my dad's name out of your mouth, because he's the best.

• **BDSM.** A common misconception about BDSM, which stands for bondage and discipline, dominance and submission, sadism and masochism, is that it's inherently degrading to those who are being dominated. After all, the person they're having sex with has tied them up, inflicted pain on them, and/or said things to them that would, outside of this context, qualify as abuse, correct? Yes, but if all parties consent to BDSM, it's understood that the "sub"—the person with their wrists bound, for example, as opposed to the person tying the knots—is the person who's really in power in this arrangement. They dictate the rules of the game: what acts are permissible, what tools are used on them, when it's time to calm things down or increase them a bit, and when the game stops. The dominator has to respect those rules, or else, yes, what they're doing is a non-consensual disobedience of their partner's boundaries, like any other sexual act that is done without permission, no matter how plain in flavor. Just because BDSM incorporates acts and objects commonly associated with violence doesn't make it violent in itself: Like any kind of "taboo" sex, it can lead to a feeling of deep recognition, trust, and affection when two or more people are able to get down and have it work for everyone involved, which can feel improbable before the first time you try it and it works. Some basic interpolations of BDSM include spanking, which has tons of crossover appeal for those who aren't as enthusiastic about BDSM. Others like to be paddled, whipped, or otherwise smacked on—although as I note in the toy story below, this doesn't have to involve any pain. Handcuffs and restraints follow the same logic.

Make a Deal

If you can't find a partner to share your fetish with, pay someone for that. There are many discreet, professional sex workers who bring home the bacon by meeting this need, and some of them work in dungeons that won't require hotel-room sneakery or the fear of someone invading your privacy at home. There is NOTHING wrong with hiring a sex worker as long as you treat the person in question with respect, and that you fully understand that they are on the job, same as if they worked at a bank. If you choose to hire a sex worker, understand the limitations of this arrangement! Escorts and other sex workers are usually paid by time, although some might have a flat rate per act. This does not mean you are purchasing them, the person, so be courteous and conscious of what they've specified the deal is. Handle the money upfront—count it in front of them and give it to them before you do anything else, and follow their boundaries and instructions to the letter. Tipping is recommended—20 percent, or $20 for every hour, at least.

ACCESSORIES TO A GREAT TIME

You don't ever "need" anything more than the corporeality you were born with to have fun sex—but you can *want* to use sex toys, or, in some people's cases, be able to orgasm only with their deft aid. Some of us might have personal tastes or physical makeups that respond to equipment-based stimulation more than skin-on-skin contact—and that's not only fine, but great to know about yourself. Equipped with that knowledge (and actual equipment), you and your partner won't be left wringing your hands in the buff, disappointed and confused as to why you *just can't come*. Opting to add sex toys to an already hot and lovely practice is usually even more of a good thing.

How to Be Suave in a Sex Store

Go to a sex store. Shop. Make a purchase or, if nothing strikes your fancy, leave. Done! Seriously, dudes: No one is judging you. The clerk is being paid by the hour and wants to go home and see what non-adult movies look good tonight—maybe order a little Italian or something. The other patrons are *also* in a sex store. You're good.

WOULDN'T IT BE FUNNY IF WE HAD THE BEST ORGASMS OF OUR LIVES?

Have a new sex-cohort you intend to kick it with for a minute or two? When you're ready to broach the subject of adding new routines to your shared sexual repertoire, empty your bedside table's drawer and invest in some new sex-based equipment, if that's what you two are into. If you're unsure and want to find out what your common stances are there, hit the sex store together. Yes: Take a romantic stroll along the walls of cock rings and scads of blow-up dolls for whom the only variable is hair color, but whose packaging makes the lewd and unconvincing promise that the delights within match exactly the experience of a carnal tryst with your most jerked-off-over celebrity.

Visiting an erotic supermarket as a couple follows the "perfect date" model, after all—it's a "joke" outing that can, surprise surprise, accelerate your blood at warp speed and find you fucking desperately in the parking lot before you know it. This is the handiwork of a dyed-in-the-wool and classic iteration of the "wouldn't it be funny if" going-out structure. Stopping into a retailer rated XXX is king of the form. You're familiar with this template, I bet. *Wouldn't it be funny if we got high and went to the planetarium?* molts to reveal its true skin: You didn't know it yet, but your actual motivation was gawping at the universe's majesty, plus that of this human comet beside you, and, bing big-bang boom, you're car-fucking. *Wouldn't it be funny if we went to that Halloween party in sheets we drew our invented, two-person cult's insignia on and insisted to everyone that it was real in the 1970s?* Oh, now you two share the furtive alliance that comes with a secret no one else is allowed to know, plus you're creating it by literally wrapping yourselves in bedclothes, aka what you regularly have sex on? How novel! Why, is that a car fuck I spy just beyond the fake-cobwebbed bushes out front? No joke is ever really a joke, and this is especially true at the sex store.

When you make your first shared venture to the grocery store with a partner, it can feel awkward: an immediate, accursed, *Oh, God, does this mean they think I want to marital-bliss it up with them or something? GAK!* hyper-commitment. Going to an adult store is that errand, depressurized, but ends up drawing you closer than considering the merits of less figurative hot dogs and cherry pies together would. (I love when gastronomic euphemisms skew super-patriotic *and* lewd.)

Even the most diplomatic of sexual tastes, however eagerly a person wants to express them, can take some time to announce themselves, as I have so often experienced firsthand. One great shortcut: Plunk yourselves in front of their accoutrements. You will find yourself Astro-gliding right over to where the wares of your SECRET INNERMOST DESIRES are housed eventually, if not with great if subconscious haste, and the same will be true of your companion. *Ha-ha, oh boy, handcuffs? What is this, a sit-com doing a "kink" episode where our prudish heroes, Larry and Linda, decide to "spice things up a little"? How hilarious would it be if we bought those?* Well, all right, but make sure to keep track of their key, or else you're going to have a strained interaction with the AAA after you're auto-erotically manacled to the steering wheel four minutes later.

You can and probably will drop the yuk-yuk pretense a few minutes into your jaunt. Going to the sex store doesn't have to masquerade as pure and simple folly—some of you are self-possessed people who don't stumble clumsily around their desire, and that rules. If you're reticent to go sex-browsing because you're worried someone will laugh at you, however: Look over there. There's a whole row of penis-shaped candy that does not appear to have a hint of novelty about it. Self-serious dick lollipops! What!!! That's hilarious. If you note the ad copy on the packaging surrounding you, the word "rod" is used in earnest *a lot.* You are in the company of a merchant who sells more *Fifty Shades of Grey* "starter kits" than everything else in the store combined. (Sex-shop employees at all different dildo-purveyors have insisted to me that this is true, and while I think it's fucking rad that so many people are inspired to step up their sexual exercises by those books and movie, I still can't quite get over seeing a rack of silver clip-on ties marketed as the height of carnality.) If you're into one of the things I poked fun at above? Guess what? I would be totally game and encouraging if we were sexual teammates and you proposed utilizing one of those things—anything new to me is also scintillating to me.

The most difficult-seeming aspect of this—the proliferation of choice—isn't even all that complex! You know how, upon being presented with the heaping rows of shelves at a bookstore when you didn't go in with a particular volume in mind, you blank out? *Jesus H. Cam'Ron, where do I start? What do I like? Do I even like ANYTHING?*

You do—abundance is just dizzying! Freak boutiques are less stultifying, in part, because the variety is winnowed: You're working with a pretty static set of categories here, and though their manufacturers have done their best to try to swindle you into thinking that the variance of bumps, speeds, colors, and shapes of a specific item will have the greatest of bearings on your ability to come, this is true only some of the time, and if you're on a budget, cheap toys are basically all the same—with some exceptions, which we'll go into in a bit.

It is imperative that you shop for your sexual toolkit in the flesh, not online, where you might not be as inclined to browse. The internet is rife with smutty weirdness, but you typically have more control over what area of that you're seeing. Let yourself be surprised! If you pick a toy that's a dud? Note what you/your person disliked about it, and on your next sex-shop spree, tell an employee, and they can help you find something more to your liking.

This past year, I was walking through the West Village in New York City, a neighborhood where window mannequins in harnesses, latex masks, and stretch teddies represent 51 percent of the population: Sex stores are *everywhere*. A person I was fond of happened to be in town, and our agreement was, *Let's try everything, as frequently as possible, save for a few acts that aren't to our tastes*. As he summarized our sex life: "We don't care who's in charge, as long as *someone's* in charge." We tried just about everything we could think of, but even sexual geniuses (like this guy was) can exhaust their mental capacities. In need of a muse in the form of a storefront mannequin wearing a chain-mail thong and pasty set, we took to the Village.

We were looking for, at least, the basics. For us, this meant: cloth restraints that attached with Velcro, a plain rubber six-inch dildo, a whip, and an uncomplicated three-speed, phallic six-inch vibrator. We made that last purchase because it's really fun for someone to pick out a new solo sex toy for you to use with them on the brain: "You know what would be hot? If you picked out the vibrator that you want me to use when I'm touching myself and thinking of you." I watched as my dude's eyes exploded, then promised him I'd send pictures of myself using it.

If you're the giver of such a gift—and this works for all genders with the sex toy of your choosing!—re-order some of the wording above. "It would be so sexy if you used this when you thought of me." The only practical alteration you might want to make here: Let the person choose the toy that reminds them of you. This *does not* mean in appearance. No good vibrators, except for super-specialized and well-crafted models made exactly to this specification, look anything like real penises, similar to how you would never confuse a Fleshlight with a vagina. They'll want to pick something that *feels* as good as you do, which could be kind of weird-looking. I have never seen a part of the human body that looks like my Hitachi Magic Wand, about which I will write and all but perform a moan-based aria in a bit.

After we stocked the pantry with these household staples, my companion in the village and I strayed over to shelves in further reaches of the store. "Have you ever tried one of these?" he asked, studying the box of an electric-shock device.

"I have, but never with you." It was added to the growing pile on the counter, along with a full-body trussing kit and a few bottles of lube, which was all we could manage before we had to split back to my apartment. Of course, we didn't quite make it: Sometimes carfucking is surreptitious cabfucking! Who knew? (We did. We did it all the time, and it was unsurpassable.)

TOOLS OF THE LAID

When it comes to the assemblage of my stockpile of sexual apparatuses, textiles, and machinery, I apply the same practicalities as when I'm shopping for clothes. If I'm picking out super-brash or unconventional-feeling pieces that I know won't make it into my regular rotation, I tend to buy cheap ones. I'm not insistent upon copping the inscrutable Tantric Master's Golden Temple Glass-Blown Staff–type goods of the sort that, despite some cost like $397 MSRP, are indistinguishable from the contents of packages with greasy hunks smiling on their cardboard backing. Though I have used expensive equipment with those who are extra-selective about their sexual accessories, my body didn't respond better to them—I just felt like a rich person for a second. This dissipated hastily. Outside of my $100+ Hitachi, sex toys in the $50-and-under range work fine for me.

I don't go for toys of unknown provenance that seem human-rights-impingingly low-cost and break on their first rodeo. I'm long past the days of picking up whatever my local head shop had on offer and calling it a day. Unless I'm in the market for something extra-specific, I favor visiting a sex-positive specialty store, like Babeland, and getting the most inexpensive kink-aids they've got on offer. Since they won't have to withstand much wear and I don't much care if they break, they don't have to cost me much.

For pieces that I know I'll be using with great regularity, like my "anchor" vibrator that lives on a hidden ledge on the side of my bed, I'm willing to invest more to guarantee that I've got something both long-lasting and exactly right for my specific needs. I spent slightly over $100 on the vibrator I've had for the past three years, and my feelings about it are such that they make me sound like a contented husband: *She's still just as beautiful as the day I met her. She still surprises me every day.* I also spend extra if a partner and I are picking out a toy to use together, like a two-way vibrator or a silicone strap-on situation.

Something More Comfortable

Though their novelty factors are unparalleled, cheap lingerie and intimates from porn stores, outside of stockings and panties (especially the edible ones, which, by the by, make for a great on-the-go snack any ol' time), are rarely good fits for anyone. I can't tell you how many balls of tangled pink ribbon and scarlet lace haunt the farthest reaches of my bureau, unworn. You usually can't try trashy lingerie on in adult emporiums, and because they're usually offered in letter sizes but include cups on the bust and also cover your waist/hip areas, it's rare to find one that actually looks like your body makes sense in it, and if a piece of clothing intended to help you feel sexy feels instead like an unflattering nuisance, you should definitely *not* buy it. Stay away unless you're fine with spending money on something that might not fit.

If you're buying lingerie for someone else at a sleaze vendor, it's even harder to guess their size. The exceptions: You can usually ballpark anything made out of fishnet or any other stretchy materials (so long as the garment in question doesn't have molded bra cups), any one-panel front-covering-type piece that's skirted and ties in the back like an apron as well as over the shoulders, and pasties are pretty intuitive.

Another rule for those browsing on behalf of their partners: The rule of sex-clothes is that, if you particularly like a certain style of clothing, shoe, or toy that your person doesn't already own, you buy it for them—the prime technique if you want to annoy me with your fetishes is to expect me to furnish them, when springing for an article of lacy fabric that I know someone is particularly into is reserved for days when I want to show them that I've gotten them a gift. If a person wants their partner to experiment with a certain utensil, or drape themselves in tawdry fabrics, footwear, or accessories of their loftiest onanistic dreams, and the desired doesn't already own that thing, the desirous party is also the purchasing one. When you're shopping for non-trashy lingerie, whether that's for yourself or your partner, invest in it as you would any other nice, formal outfit, and go to a specialty store.

What follows is a list of the collection of products I keep in my bedside drawer, how I choose each object, and discussion of the various offshoots of each that I've used, too. This is only a tiny excerpt of all the sex toys on offer for those looking for suggestions about where to begin:

• **Lubricant.** This is another area where a higher investment pays off, since nothing wrecks my momentous enjoyment of whatever lascivious thing I need extra wetness for than gummy, sticky K-Y Jelly. I find that gross lube also puts off newcomers when it comes to acts that require it. It's supremely unhelpful, when you're trying to establish something as awesome, normal, and totally not a big deal, to involve a slimy, tacky-feeling substance in those things.

Though amateurish moves like that can be appealing in their own right, I'm more inclined to focus on making a person feel good as best I know how. My favorite lube is the water-based ID Glide, which feels sleek against skin and is compatible with latex condoms and silicone sex toys. Water-based is usually best, regardless of what brand you pick up: Though silicone lubes are definitely the silkiest, I recommend them only if you're not incorporating sex toys into your encounters, since their active ingredient can corrode the silicone or other synthetics your tools are made of. I stay away from oil-based lubricants altogether—they weaken condoms, can stain sheets, clothes, and toys, and feel like grease. The most utilitarian lube investment you can make: A bottle of silicone lube, 250 ml or bigger, will last you for a long-ass time and is economical, since you can get one for under $20 if you're scrupulous.

• **Dildos.** Though there's a vast world of fake dicks to explore, one utilitarian crowd-pleaser is a six-inch hollow silicone phallus. If you're using this kind of toy to explore anal activities, you might prefer something smaller (or larger). These come in rubber, jelly, glass, and all kinds of other materials—pay attention to what yours is made of, what kind of lubricant it's compatible with, and if it needs any special cleansers. Smaller toys follow the same guidelines.

• **Two-person toys.** Since items designed for simultaneous usage can serve myriad different wants and needs, talk to your person before springing for one. Browse all the different options together: Do you both want to be penetrated at once? Does one of you want to remotely command the toy pleasuring the other (e.g., operate a vibrating egg)? Invest in a quality product that you can agree on. Picking out a specialized toy together is super-sexy: You're harboring and employing what feels like secret sexual contraband, and there is pretty much nothing hotter than that.

• **Strap-on harnesses.** These can be used as a part of bondage, but it's also common that people without dicks belt them around their hips in order to accommodate a hands-free. It's a good idea to purchase this at the same time you do the toy you intend to use it with to guarantee a fit, but if not, measure the circumference of your dick before you pick one of these, and shop accordingly.

• **Ball gags.** Outside of my color preferences for these (black or red, please), the various ones I've used were pretty uniform in terms of how they felt and looked, although if you get off on these specifically, there are more sophisticated-looking models for your enjoyment. For the rest of us: Go cheap, because these are basically interchangeable.

• **Rope.** Rope is rope. Nylon and cotton weaves are both great for bondage. Get it at the hardware store, why don't you—that makes it feel extra fucked-up and hot.

• **Ben wa balls.** These are strings or sets of spheres most commonly made of steel. They are inserted into an orifice for "training" said part of the body: The person accepting them is supposed to clench their muscles around the weights, which vary in size, in order to train their control of that part of their body. Since Ben wa balls are essentially just heavy metal circles, you don't have to be too picky.

• **Whips, crops, and paddles.** My favorites of this category are more bark than bite. Sex stores sell plenty of these that don't hurt outside of the tiniest pleasant stinging, no matter how hard (and how loudly) they hit your skin. Ask about it! You can try them for yourself at many places, albeit on the palms of your hands instead of your butt.

• **Restraints.** You can get cuffs made of fabric or sturdier materials for wrists, ankles, or a person's entire body. These include handcuffs, elaborate bondage systems that render a person motionless, and chains, and can be used by themselves or to bind a person to a bed or other area. Anything that restricts a person's motion counts.

- **Bondage tape.** After you're done in the rope aisle of your local home improvement emporium, pick a wide roll made of PVC so that it doesn't run the risk of tugging at your skin or hair—it should adhere mostly to itself.
- **Blindfolds.** Unless you specifically like a certain shape or material for these: You can use the one you got on your last flight, or underwear, or a scarf, or basically any cloth you want. But use underwear.

ELECTRIC LADY

My first vibrator came from that most ennobled of mall smut-gateways, the crass chain-emporium of trucker hats and dreadful novelty shot glasses known as Spencer's Gifts. Spencer's gift to teenage-me was my first assured source for regular orgasms, after my first girlfriend and I picked up matching dough-colored six-inchers on a lark. They ran on two AAs and pluck, and I burned mine out within three months. I worked through several more cylindrical cheapos, all battery-operated and built to crash, in the next seven months before deciding to pick a more sustainable option because I adore the environment and care deeply about climate change (read: yes, those things, but also my access to quick, low-effort climaxin').

The first contender was, as recommended by the guttural titterings of my collegiate dining-hall companions, the luckless Rabbit model. I hit up Babeland, one of my favorite sex stores exactly because it's so unsexy, to try it out—when I say it leaves me cold, imagine a benevolent-looking person with a calm demeanor and asymmetrical haircut pressing a writhing bit of silicone against your palm and saying, as though prescribing you medicine, "The level of pressure is perfect for the average G-spot." The warty-surfaced Rabbit was not for me, and not just because of the way it was pitched—it just didn't feel right.

Vibrator preferences vary from person to person. Some aspects of a vibrator you might prioritize: speed, intensity of vibration, sound level, texture, waterproofness, length, width, and/or the availability of compatible attachments. I like earthquake-grade tremors, and I like them fast. Concentrated vibrations are like the "tight pussy" of the clitoral stimulation world: Unless a person specifically does NOT like it, it's customarily a crowd favorite.

I look for toys that do that first and foremost, and then consider which of other criteria I'll compromise on or account for in order to pick an accessory that fulfills my most legs-pressed-together needs. Having done research beforehand, I asked the Babeland employee about a vibrator I had heard didn't come to play around, the Hitachi Magic Wand. She pulled out what looked like a half sonogram wand, half white microphone, except twice the size of either—it had a circular, softish head, a simple-looking black switch on its side, and a corded end. It *looked* unsexy, and as we talked about it, I had some questions: I was supposed to hitch myself to an outlet each and every time I wanted to masturbate with it? *Yes.* There's no setting on which it's quieter than a whole landscaping company's fleet of lawn mowers growling in unison... meaning I would have to be discreet about when I used it? *Nah, it's just that loud.* Oh my god, that's the LOW setting? *Yeah, now put out your other hand and I'll show you the higher speed.* WHOA. THIS IS GOING TO BE MY RIDE-OR-DIE FOREVER, HUH? *Yeah...yeah, it is.*

The Hitachi Magic Wand is phenomenal used by myself or with any number of lovely assistants, but when it comes to using vibrators with partners, I either put this behemoth away or use it in tandem with something that can be inserted comfortably into them or me—or both. If you're easing into this whole concept, you can choose a small vibrator, or super-controllable ones, like finger vibrators—these slip on like fingertip rings and can go into whatever orifices your hands would without them, or intensify *any* kind of touching.

ROUTINE MAINTENANCE

I like to clean my vibrator three times a month if I'm using it alone, plus after every new partner. I think this is a pretty good rule for toys that don't involve penetration—and in those cases, I clean them nearly every time I use 'em. All-natural disinfecting wipes are good for stuff taken vaginally, but I give anything involving anal the full top-down scrub.

Check the packaging for the materials used to make your sex toy: If it's silicone or Pyrex through and through, you can boil it submerged in a pot of water for three or so minutes, and you're all good. Alternatively, you can even wash it in a dishwasher if it has a hot-water setting, so this can easily become a regular part of your tidying-up routine. ("To Do: Vacuum. Wash windows. Remember to load vibrator next to the dirty plates.") If there are electrical elements, use the next method, avoiding the parts that might be damaged or could shock ya when met with cleaning solvent on them.

Toys with porous bases or elements like "jelly" (extra-squishy-feeling and pliable material) or rubber are as attracted to bacteria as you are to using them. For this reason, I typically don't stock these myself, but if a partner likes them and wants to use them together, I ask that, if it's an impromptu thing and we haven't picked out a new one together, we use a toy cleaner, or, if they don't have it, some other kind of disinfectant, since the chemicals in soaps, especially scented ones, can be absorbed into the toy and cause infections upon contact with skin.

For toys of glass, plastic, or other kinds of non-porous substances: Use a disposable cloth like a paper towel, or a clean rag, with antibacterial spray or soap and warm water, to shine up your dildo or whatever. Household tasks can be so tedious!!!

For all other materials, check the packaging—substances that are designed to verisimilarly imitate human skin, like that on anatomical reproductions or sex dolls, usually require special care.

THE REPLACEMENTS

Sometimes, toys need to be retired if they're too far gone to rinse up in the dishwasher and return to your bed good as new. (The upside to this time of mourning and loss: Now you get to replace them with new ones!)

Any machine with an electrical flaw, or a corroded battery compartment, should be removed from your collection. TRUST ME ON THIS ONE—I learned this via sparks flying out of a vibrator and straight onto a sensitive area, and I do not recommend it. If the engine in your toy wears out, or if it starts chomping batteries like handfuls of candy underwear, bid it adieu, as it is likely on the road to faulty wiring. Visible dents or flaws in most toys are fine as long as they don't affect its structure or how it feels on/in you.

There's one situation in which I junk toys regardless of quality-control concerns: If I split with a long-term partner, with whom I used toys specifically together and not so much by myself, I offer them the toys or throw them away, even when I want to employ them with someone new. My Hitachi is a one-on-one thing that enjoys the occasional threesome, but any equipment purchased specifically for me and one other partner is out. I don't want my next paramour, whenever it is that they come on the scene, to immediately feel expectations from me based on what I did with an old squeeze, and especially not in the context of our forays into non-standardized sex as they're unfolding in real time. I don't mean to bestow upon some stained hunks of suggestively shaped metal and rubber some kind of sacrosanct and solemn *Great Meaning*, so if you and your partner are like, "Actually, it's fine with me that that piece has known other orifices," go ahead and do you. Just make sure everything in your toolkit is clean.

PARTNER SEX

For those who are shacking up, settling down, or just transfixed by their partners: Having a long-term love in your life is as privileged and special an experience as using the bottom half of your body as a divining rod pointed all over the ol' singles bar. (What is a "singles bar," guys? Is it a fantasy invention of 1970s radio?) You get to cram your affection, respect, and attraction into one sweet vessel, and be expanded (and turned on) by theirs. Sex, when you're in love, is hot as hellfire—and when it's not, that's okay, too. To a point—as long as it's not purgatory.

How *ominous*, I know! Be at peace, my besotted. A happy partnership does not transpire only if you have coruscating sex each time you get in bed. You don't even need to be physically intimate with a partner to be contented with their company (and this extends even to long-term relationships). Finding someone who is your preternaturally ideal sexual match, and who *also* makes charming conversation with your most irritating colleagues, listens to you bemoan your parents' myriad failings, thinks decently, and conscientiously remembers what you get on your hot dogs without having to ask twice (SWOON), is probably not something anyone should expect from a realistic coupledom. (Still, I am never going to settle for less, hee.)

This does not mean you have to hunker down for a peaceful life of quilting and clandestine masturbation. If you are part of a loving, but sexually lacking, couple: LUCKY YOU; I'm serious. It means you have the trust in place to potentially experience the heart- (and orgasm-) reactivating phenomenon of having your sexual relationship with your person ascend in quality as you pass more and more time together—instead of the other way around— as long as you make a verbal point of setting it on a new course.

Maybe in some long-term relationships, you feel or have felt like, *God, the sex was unmatched in the beginning, and now I'm more attracted to the relish all over this footlong*? (Ew, not like that! I should have picked a different food. Maybe outside of Eros and Thanatos, Freud wasn't a hack? Nah, wait...*[thinks about his probings of his teenage daughter]*...he totally was. Oh, did you wonder why we're mostly not employing the work of that greasy cokeball in this book?) Whether you start out utterly compatible or not, there are going to be valleys as you make the long journey of traversing your sexual peaks. Then you get to climb out of them together by finding all-new ways to fuck each other stupid.

When I notice that a partner and I are in one of those subaltern places, it doesn't presage the end of us. Even if I've been with a person many times, one of us can always opt to remodel how that goes, whether that's by changing one element of the sex or a top-down renovation. Given the fact that it would probably be quite startling if one of you showed up in a pleather-and-cellophane catsuit one day if that wasn't already your norm, you don't have to make a sudden and dramatic overture if it's forced, or that you feel wouldn't be well-received without easing in to your ideas more subtly first. While there are plenty of bonuses to updating your wardrobe with complicated sex garments of synthetic origin (and maybe you feel that shocking your person would be just the thing), there are less dramatic ways to surprise the person you relish most.

What's wonderful about extended hangouts with other people that hinge heavily on trust: You're used to talking about difficult-feeling topics of all stripes (such as openhearted discussions pertaining to your lunatic upbringing and hatred of sauerkraut). What makes you think *your* person won't be receptive to hearing out your questions and concerns—in the style of a restaurant comment card, except way more loving—about whether they're enjoying what you do when you're spending time together horizontally, as well? That's how you should frame this conversation at its outset.

The feedback here, *unlike* that on a pink index card at TGI Friday's, should be reciprocal and symbiotic, like everything else you do together. It is entirely disingenuous-feeling to talk about your own sexual needs by saying, "I think YOU could be happier," then strapping on your new bodysuit and insisting that they love it, so that's not what you're about here. You're in a relationship, so you know how it feels to consider someone else's mindset when you're making decisions that affect both of you. You know that happiness comes from asking them what they need to find a level of mutual satisfaction that at least borders on "Strongly Agree."

The benefits of hearing how your person thinks independently about the sex life you're cohabiting are prodigious. Chief among these: You can adjust how you care for and account for them in both physical and love-based ways upon hearing them out. Also crucial: Listening to their characterization of the sex you two have before interjecting with your own analysis means that you are getting their true opinion on the matter—not one tempered by yours. You could make the case that YOU, then, are the one who won't be proffering the truth of your heart, but that's fake. You will go into this conversation knowing what you're looking to express to your person—the inner honesty of what you're looking for won't change based on the one announced across the table from you. If you don't fit the conversation into the framework of what YOU want, both parts of your duo have the opportunity to express their real feelings, but if you do, they might want to adjust their feelings to cater to your happiness, because they love you and want you to have nice things, whether those are accented by condoms or condiments. Well, TOO BAD, sweet and kind partner of yours!! You want the same thing for their caring ass, which means making sure they are heard in full.

Here's how to go about talking openly about this, even if you're skittish: Don't feel any pressure to make this particular conversation SULTRILY SIMMER with passionate Don Juan–style suaveness. If it ends up turning you both on, that's very fortunate, and you should get thee atop of the other person with haste, but trying to engineer that outcome is unfair to both of you: Setting this talk up as a sensuous tête-à-tête puts pressure on both

of you to live up to what the other person wants when you're trying to figure out what that is in the first place. But it's not quite a
staid State of the Union, either; talking about sex with someone in
super-dry terminology can make me feel like I am being strangled
by a pair of sensible khakis. What you're hoping for is a tone that
lands somewhere between the two, which it most likely will if you
like and are willing to be upfront with each other.

Some factors to assess before you start chattering away about
your junk: Do you have guaranteed privacy for at least an hour?
Rather than being mad stressed out about the Stevenson account
or an upcoming deadline or what have you, is your person's face
relaxed in an unburdened configuration of calmness (that you are
about to fuck up)? Have you, moments ago, been told that now
is not a good time to have sex, and you're seeking justice and
retribution by springing a conversation about how to bone properly on them? (I have been this guy and regret it a lot—don't do
this.)

If you have checked off boxes reading Y, Y, and DUDE, N, to
the preceding questions about your experience today, say, "Hey—
I've been thinking lately—do you mind if we talk? I know that
sounds mad serious, but I promise everything's okay with us on
my end," or whatever non-automated version of that template
sounds normal coming out of your mouth. If the answer is N,
WHAT'S UP?, say, "I know this is going to seem like it's coming
from out of nowhere, but I want to make sure you're happy with
the sex we've been having lately. Is there anything else I could be
doing for you?" Keep eye contact, and don't affect a funereal tone
of voice—treat this like *no big deal, just assessing the current
of our shared sexual wellness, who even cares, anything good
come in the mail today?* I find that partners like to try to out-calm
each other if someone sets that precedent. It's like a reverse yell-
ing match: "YOU WANT RESPECTFUL, OPEN COURTESY?
[whispers] I'll give you respectful, open courtesy!!!" *[sits and listens patiently before reacting]*.

If your person demurs, say, "You know you can always talk

to me about it if there is something, right?" and keep your mouth closed in an encouraging smile directed at them for a few beats. If they choose to follow this up with something significant: Follow the model of our inverted scream-a-thon just above, and don't take ANY of it as a pointed critique of your inherent sexual worthiness, even if your partner says, "This is a pointed critique of your inherent sexual worthiness." In that case, dump the jerk. Otherwise, you might be surprised by what your partner tells you they've been liking/disliking about wanting more/less of, or secretly hoping to introduce to your sexual co-membership's repertoire. *Toe parties?!? You thought you knew them so well!* You did, and now you know them even better!—and that you might want to invest in a pedicure (and men: you know it's totally normal for you to get these, too, right?).

Ask questions. Is your partner stoked on your current ratio of sexual congress per day/week/month/half hour/eon/whatever seems most appropriate to your situation? Is there anything they're hoping to try, but *didn't maybe sorta feel that the right time to bring it up had yet happened*? (Aw, whatta waffler. That time is now!!) What sex acts do they like most, and when do they feel best? HOLD EYE CONTACT. THINK ABOUT THE MAIL. YOU ARE DOING THE MATURE AND KIND THING HERE.

Once they've expelled all they've been keeping, get the point across that you're grateful about that. Then continue, "I wanted to talk to you about how I'm feeling, too." Let them know how you feel about all of the aforementioned, and what potential adjustments you two might want to make. Once you've finished, ask what they think without interrupting their answers. I am willing to wager the other person will not be SHOCKED and APPALLED about a sexual lull they can not only already tell you're bored by, but agree is an issue of their own volition.

If this still seems like A LOT to discuss with your person because you two haven't adroitly broached the topic of sex until now, imagine how they're feeling. Remember that they didn't have the stability of advance warning and agency in this conversation, as you did. If they seem freaked out, don't forsake your respectful, open courtesy by rising to meet the pitch of their emotional tenor, because that gets everybody exactly NOWHERE besides possibly primed to hurt each other. How you do this: Be sure of this conversation as a worthy and loving endeavor, because it is. *Dilige et quod vis fac* = especially significant when you're trying to handle the person that you love most with care.

GROUP SEX ETIQUETTE

Threesomes are one of life's greatest pleasures, ranking alongside glacially cold seltzer, seeing a baby skunk in the wild, and the poetry of Guillaume Apollinaire. *That* good.

There are many groupings, roles, and shapes in which you can enjoy them: I have been the special guest star as well as part of the host couple plenty of times, in differently gendered lineups, and left each bizarre love triangle with a song in my heart and exhausted mouth-muscles. Group sex is like reading an Apollinaire poem about a baby skunk WHILE guzzling a crispy Schweppes. That good.

A threesome with three breathing beings, two of whom are involved for longer than just that night, usually has to be artfully assembled. Group sex, when it involves a long-term couple, can veer into gruesomeness if you're dealing with delicate personalities—which is to say, "personalities." The biggest challenge of ménage-à-triangles for those in relationships is the fact that you have to account for and manage not only your and one other partner's happiness, which is strenuous enough on its own, but that of another person forming all-new angles in this shape. Each person involved is CAUTION—FRAGILE, because threesomes can feel like ego wrecking balls even if they're handled with the softest of kid gloves.

When they aren't? You know how it's rude to insert sidebars

into conversations with three or more people that you know only you and one other person in the group will get? Imagine that same ill-mannered behavior, except naked. Nobody likes to feel neglected, or extrapolate that into butchered self-esteem. I am happy to say I've never experienced that, but that is, in large part, because I would never become involved in a threesome that I foresaw was an emotional demolition derby disguised as the kind of agreeable fuckfest that I wondered about from pornography.

Asking the person to whom you are committed to have a threesome with you might feel daunting if you're monogamous with them. This doesn't mean it is impossible, or that they'll shoot you down out of hand. If you're uncertain whether your person will respond favorably to a three-part harmony, do some detective work. Just maybe don't do it by saying, "Hey! You know your friend Dan from the radio show with the graceful hands and shag-carpet chest hair? I want to lobotomize him via fucking his brains out. Wanna join in, person I love?" This approach is obviously a bad one, but let's dissect just how it would result in watching your their-place toothbrush get snapped over your partner's knee:

1. It suggests a specific person. In addition to the above principles regarding who gets to pick, and why, in terms of the two of you: How do you know Dan would be down? If it's because you asked him firsthand, you likely extracted that information via a proposition that your person would hate. You either dangled the prospect of a threesome without their permission, or you said, "Hey, DAN. DANIEL. HEY. Over here, behind the turntables. Real quick secret: I desperately want you to bend me over. No, Matt doesn't know, but he could watch if he wanted, I guess?" or you didn't even mention Matt at ALL, until now, when you confirmed to him that you and his colleague are making flimsy passes at each other behind his back. That's insulting. Don't do it. If you DON'T know Dan would be down, then you're confounding this whole situation for a prospect that is unlikely to go down with the exact cast of characters you were hoping in reality, since finding

willing and enthusiastic threesome partners is...complex. More on that later. First, I'm going to keep berating you for not saying something that I myself wrote! *How could you???*

2. It introduces aspects of what you're attracted to in others, which your partner's brain may translate as, "What I'm not giving you." The qualities you admire in Dan and so callously brought up, like a jerk, I would never think like that—lithe hands, Travolta-level fur-pecs—are a fun path for your person to follow straight to spiraltown: *Oh, God, is she saying she thinks my hands look so stumpy they're practically feet and also that male-pattern baldness, chest edition, is now a thing I'm nervous about re: my body??? How come I never knew how hideous I was?* In actuality, you would never be this wrongheaded in your thinking, but specifying any characteristic of someone you might like to give a tour of your shared bedroom should be vague, outside of—and maybe even including—their gender.

3. It frames what you're proposing as something you (and Dan) will be doing ALONE. It's important to specify that it's about the two of you, rather than an exclusionary party zone you and Matt get to share as a part of your affection for each other. Though threesomes...wait for this mind-blowing revelation...involve someone outside your relationship, they're (mostly) all about the two of you in the long-term. Matt is agreeing to try something you've expressed will make you happy, and you're rewarding Matt by showing him why that was a good idea, via incredibly hot sex, rather than a grave misjudgment. "I want to get fucked by another person" makes no mention of the fact that your partner is in the picture.

The two predominant fears when it comes to group sex are jealousy and exclusion. Once you've worked out that each party is willing, take care of the following and you've got very little to be afraid of:

• In couples, the suggester lets the suggestee pick the third— and, without a couple's encouragement, a third probably shouldn't

ask at all. If you're asking for a threesome, your main collaborator gets to pick the featured guest. This is the rule even if your girlfriend is giving you one "for your birthday," which is kind of a harsh toke from the outset—does she *want* to do it, or is she feeling pressured into making you happy "this one time" by wincing through something she's uncomfortable with? It could easily be the opposite: She wants to do it, but is self-conscious about that fact, so she's got to wrap it in a bow—much like when I get loved ones expensive caramels as gifts because I know they'll open and eat them WITH me.

Pointing out an object of your affections can get someone's guard up because it invites instantaneous self-comparison, which is something you want to AVOID as much as possible, for your sake and your triangle's. It's going to be difficult enough when you're sizing up a person's naked flesh as measured against your own, or when your person is, so don't invite that beauty contest as you broach the idea to begin with. Suggesting a third could also lead your person to believe you've been harboring a sexual or romantic YEARNING for your intended, which is . . . not that cool to think about, if you've been actively boning and/or adoring someone who, the whole time, has been wanting to bone/adore someone other than you. Not that there's anything wrong with wanting to fuck/love two or more people at once! There isn't. But don't bring your main person into it unless they want that, don't fuck/love around on them if you're monogamous, and if you find yourself YEARNING instead of being present in your current relationship, open or not: Consider ending it.

• **Do not assume a person wants to have a threesome with you because they've done so with others.** It's of the highest importance that you make sure every member of a threesome *knows* what's up beforehand. Picture it: You're headed over to your couple-friends' house for a cassoulet and some Hpnotiq. (Excuse me; I am just constructing the dream life that I hope with all of me that you actually enjoy in reality.) *Everything is normal!* you think—or don't, because you never think that thought when life actually is.

Instead, you settle in for some light gin rummy and heavy drinking of same, plus whatever bioluminescent liqueur you brought.

All of a sudden, you feel a hand trailing across your ankle, which is crossed elegantly above your knee with only the slightest ring of skin showing above your loafer. You're so startled that your shoe's pristinely shined penny pinwheels across the linoleum—you've jerked your leg back hard enough to dislodge it.

"What the fuck?" you demand, eyes ponging back and forth between the two possible offenders.

"Sorry—we thought you were down with threesomes?"

You 52-pick-up the cards and, in your disbelief and anger, throw the deck at the Ming vase they've (cleverly, you have to admit) fashioned into a bong, smashing it. How dare they! Just because you had glancingly mentioned a pleasant evening you recently passed in a threesome doesn't mean you are CONSTANTLY open to getting boned in tandem all the time! How assumptive, rude, and card-game-destroyingly bland of them.

I have been in this exact position—well, save for the gin rummy (but not the Hpnotiq)—and I felt disrespected and unconsidered. The couple in question were some girls I knew, and whose nascent friendship I enjoyed, from hanging out at this one dance party we all frequented on Monday nights. The thing that sometimes sucks about taking a relaxed approach to group sex, and having it present itself in the strands of friendly conversation, is that people try to Simon Says you into a threesome without your consent because they see you as a point of entry. Barf.

That behavior roundly munches sewage...but I get its incentive. If a person has intimated they love the sonorous musicality that often comes with *playin' the triangle*, a complex, beautiful genre their audience has long considered beyond the reaches of its talent, it might be tempting to ask them for lessons. That's fine! The pivotal point of that sentence, though, is the word "ask." Would you demand that a known triangle solo artist whip out their wand and give the virtuoso performance of a lifetime with nary an inkling's notice? No, you have never done that—you're not that rude.

Don't expect a threesome of someone solely because you know, or are guessing, that they have had one before. Don't expect a threesome of someone even if you've had it with the same configuration of people before! People's angles are less rigid than those found in geometry. You are not treating that person as a person, which is the most essential part of the approach to group sex in general: No one is anyone's sexy attaché. Everyone has the right to say what their limitations are not only during, but before.

• **In an intergender couple, the person of the same identity (if there is one) as the person being asked does the actual asking.** Sorry: This suggestion feels archaic. But there's a lot to be said for considering the perspectives and experiences of your target, then deploying whichever member of the home team might relate to them most closely. I like having one person act as the amanuensis and point of communication for both others, and that person should be the one whom the other two trust, collectively, the most—across the interpersonal board, and as applied singularly to this situation.

This can speak to a diffuse range of considerations: Maybe the third has known one of the players in question since goontimes, or perhaps shares a CSA with another. Most commonly, though, this is going to boil down to good old-fashioned gender essentialism. When I'm closer with the male figure of an equation, I am persuaded that a situation is cool, on the level, and a potentially entertaining passage of a Thursday evening when the female arm of a twosome reaches out to me. Since we're going to be, for a time, body doubles playing an at least somewhat similar role, no matter how disparate our interpretations of it, I want to know that we're countrywomen—that we're each heading into the threesome knowing what the other's deal is, and how to make her feel good and psychically protected. If you are all three of diverse, or identical, genders, go ahead and dispatch the person who speaks to them most effortlessly about how wild the ninth grade was, or this week's CSA selection of root vegetables, or whatever point of connection you've decided is basis enough for a bout of group sex. (Both topics have worked fine for me in the past.)

• **Do it with ANOTHER couple.** Having sex with another allied force means that everyone is approaching the four-way with just as much to lose!! Hee, I kid—look at it the other way, and you are viewing it correctly. Empathy will come more easily to a couple in your same romantic situation, and *close* friends might be more considerate of one another's feelings and careful not to homewreck your shit.

• **Three strangers or loose acquaintances are least messy after the fact.** I *love* a threesome comprising three randeaux. There are no lingering love-politics about which to have Serious Check-Ins (aka the WORST part of relationships, even though I know it's, yes, necessary and healthy—hard conversations are the vegetables of romance). Each and all parties are equal, and equally ready to party.

• **In any case: GET KINDA DRUNK.** But not too drunk, doye.

• **A note on asking a previously platonic friend to take part in a threesome:** You're always going to face some risk of offending someone when you make a pass at them. A unilateral truth: That risk winnows when you hint at your interest and gauge if the other person reciprocates it with genuine curiosity and levelheadedness (rather than going, "Oh, he smiled back—SHAGADELIC").

If they're freaked out? They have the right to be surprised, but they also have to respect your sexual *realité* as much as you do theirs, so end the conversation if they decide that a cool way to respond is by insulting or berating you. I have never had that happen, and I hope you don't either!

• **A note to special guest stars:** The key to nailing your walk-on role in someone else's relationship: It's best not to try and steal the show here. While this is a fun and light evening for YOU, the people with whom you're sleeping are going to maintain joint custody over this memory for the rest of the time they're magnetized to each other. While it's up to them how they approach your encounter—there's no way to control other people's feelings—you have some responsibility to contribute to its emotional tenor. How are these two treating each other? Are they looking at each other with great devotion and intensity? Don't try to hop in on that. I'm thinking of the words "equal" and "equitable." Wreathe both parties with affection and attention equally: Make all parties feel sexy, included, and accounted for. Ménagin' is the best—have fun.

OPEN RELATIONSHIPS

One method of maintaining a loving partnership that includes sex from outside forces: non-monogamy. I'm not at all proud to admit that I've cheated on almost every boyfriend I've ever had except for a few, including my last one—although that doesn't mean I stopped hooking up with other people when we were dating. The difference is, in that relationship, my foremost love associate knew about (and was cool with) my liaisons. It's taken me a while to admit this, but in the past few years I've come to accept that I mostly prefer romantic relationships that don't require me to be sexually faithful. I think a lot of people find this "deviant" or weird, but, unlikely as it may sound, it's actually not that complicated.

Monogamy has always been hard for me, even in the context of loving, committed relationships. In the past, the trouble usually began after a few months, when some new heartthrob would swim into my life. Although I knew my then-boyfriends wouldn't be cool with it, I would start lying about how often I saw said heartthrobs, flirting with them on Facebook and in person, or secretly having "sleepovers" with them that involved a lot of physical contact but no official "fooling around." I rationalized all of this behavior as *friends bein' friendly*, even though my motivations were decidedly less pure.

Once I started being dishonest, it was hard for me to stop. Although my cheating usually didn't involve anything more serious than some furtive makeout sessions, I'd always wake up the next morning smothered in guilt, which quickly morphed into resentment: Why should I feel bad about wanting to fool around with people while I'm young? The answer, of course, was BECAUSE YOU ARE LYING TO A PERSON WHO CARES ABOUT YOU, JERKUS. But I also had a point: It's totally okay to feel like kissing basically everybody, if you can find a way to do it without being deceitful and/or disrespectful to anyone else. I just hadn't figured out that way yet.

In one such monogamous relationship, which included a lengthy and serious engagement, I vowed not to cheat, and I didn't. But after two and a half years, I started backsliding into the realm of backdoor Facebook encounters. When I caught myself typing double entendres to people whose profile pictures I found achingly cute, I broke up with my then-fiancé rather than violate his trust, which I could tell I was about to do.

Even though I was the one who chose to end that relationship, I was overwhelmed by despair and grief when it was over. I wondered if I would ever be able to love someone without emotionally fucking them over with my constant tail-chasing and tomcatting, and I decided the answer was no: I had tried my hardest with someone I was prepared to spend the rest of my life with, and I had failed. Clearly I was incapable of curbing my desire to freaq a sizable fraction of the world's population, and that, I felt, made me worthy of contempt.

Then I met Wes. We were introduced by a mutual friend on a beach trip two years ago, when I was twenty-one, right before I made the choice to leave my fiancé. A few months after we settled into our partnership, Wes told me that he knew he wanted to go out with me when, upon being picked up at my apartment, I burst into the car and greeted him by affectionately biting his arm. Suave, right? That sense of sexy intrigue intensified for both of us over the course of the afternoon as we discovered we had the same favorite animal (squid) and compared our imitations of the director Orson Welles. We separated from the rest of the group for a while, and I told him secrets that not even my best friends knew at the time, like why my engagement was ending (and that it was even ending at all). I felt closer to him than I had to anyone else in a long time.

I broke up with my fiancé not long after that day. Even though wanting to be with Wes wasn't the reason behind that split, I'd be lying if I said I wasn't totally jazzed when we started dating a few weeks later. Despite the intense bond I felt with him, I tried to keep things super-casual for a few months, during which time I refused to call him my boyfriend and dated other people. I didn't want to get too involved because, as I told him one morning after we'd spent the night together, I didn't believe in the whole "love" thing. He told me that he was a longtime cheater, too, and, like me, he felt some shame about that, but he didn't think it exempted us from falling in love with each other, which, yo, we totally were! We mutually decided that non-monogamy was the best option for us as a couple, and I'm so glad we did, because it worked better than anything either of us had experienced before. And guess what? I was very incorrect about love not being real, which is probably the greatest thing I've ever been proven wrong about.

Here's what non-monogamy meant for us: Like many people who are deeply obsessed with their main squeeze, as I was with Wes, I wanted to spend as much time with him as I possibly could without our driving each other crazy. Also like many others who are deeply in love with their person, I occasionally wanted to french people who weren't him, as did he with not-mes. The difference between monogamous relationships and our thing was that we acted on those feelings, and we didn't want to sob, scream, or murk each other afterward. There was none of the sinking dread involved with cheating that I was all too familiar with. I got all of the action, with none of the harrowing doubt about whether I'd ever be able to truly love someone without fucking them over. Doesn't that sound kind of nice?

There are some drawbacks to non-monogamy, of course. I was happy with the mechanics of my romantic situation, but that doesn't mean others in my life agreed with my choices. Maybe you're one of those people, in which case, get bent! Just kidding, my dude—I like you just the same, and I'm going to do my best to clear up any misconceptions or stigmas that you, a person who is maybe curious about open relationships but skeptical that they can work, might be harboring. The truth is that it's more than possible to be in such a relationship without having it wreck your life, and that wanting to try non-monogamy doesn't make you a misguided perv who doesn't understand how to do love "right." For your perusal, I now present this not-comprehensive but still probably kind of helpful list of things worth knowing when you're figuring out how to screw the world without screwing up your relationship.

• **Don't feel like you need to "identify," but feel free to check out places where people do.** I've never identified as a "polyamorous person" or involved myself in communities based on a shared rejection of monogamy—I don't like to assign names to anything about my love life, period—but if I had to pick a descriptor for my situation, "non-monogamous" probably fits best. I'm just not that into the identity-based language I've seen used by other non-monoggos (ooh, I'm kind of into this newfound term after typing it just now—it sounds like something the Flintstones would eat).

This is not to disparage "polyamorous" or what have you communities—I understand that the big city where I live, and my friends in it, afford me the comfort of knowing others who happen to also be non-monoggo (sticking with this prehistoric delicacy), and that giving a name to any non-mainstream thing you do can help you find others who are into it wherever you are. Polyamory, which most often refers to having more than one long-term partner at a time, mostly isn't what I do—but continued blessings to anyone who chooses that.

To say I was in an "open relationship" also feels like a misnomer, because, although I'm talking about it publicly here in the service of this book, for the most part, my bond with Wes was private—we were in love, and our particular love was occupied by only the two of us. We kept our extracurricular sex casual—it never impacted the inside jokes he and I made about our stupid-looking cat, or the way we confided in each other about the stuff we were scared of as kids, or how we always seemed to want to do the same things at the same time (narrowing our eyes at crosswords at the diner, playing Boggle, performing impromptu Roy Orbison duets—everything) without talking about it first.

In writing this, I also briefly imagined how hilariously inappropriate it would be if I called myself a SWINGER, a word that makes me feel kind of like someone's aggressively mystical aunt who dresses exclusively in clothing that could be characterized as "flowing," or like the boastful, hot tub–dwelling LOVERS from *Saturday Night Live* who force stories of their earthy, open lovemaking onto everyone they meet. You're just not ever gonna catch me waxing poetic in some mineral spring about the fact that I sleep around because I think I'm a more spiritually—and oh-so-sensually—enlightened being than everyone else! My life is totally quotidian 'n' normal to me, and I don't need to make a show of this part of it or ask for permission to have it feel valid/okay that I adore being a total Runaround Sue. For me, it's all very "I woke up like this (in someone else's bed)."

There are lots of other non-monogamous permutations, from marriage-like unions among a group of people to "monogamish" situations, a term coined by the sex advice columnist Dan Savage that refers to situations in which a couple is mostly monogamous, but give each other leeway for occasional extracurricular fun, either together or separately.

• **Set clear ground rules with your partner.** Being upfront with each other about what you can and can't do outside of the time you spend together is hands down the most important factor in maintaining an open relationship—like, the whole point of non-exclusive arrangements is to absolve yourselves of the deception and guilt that come with "cheating." I think starting a relationship with the understanding that you'd like it to be non-monogamous is probably far easier than trying to open a monogamous relationship, but the template for bringing the subject up is the same either way. Saying, like, "GUESS WHAT? I want to fool around with other people!! Fun, right?" is a great way to hurt somebody's feelings, put them on the defensive, and/or make them think that you're not attracted to them anymore. Instead, start by telling your partner why committing (or staying committed) to each other is a priority for you (e.g., "I love being with you in all ways, so I don't want you to think that what I'm about to tell you means I'm not into you anymore. I'm bringing this up because our relationship is important to me, and I want it to last for a long time"). Then explain how you're feeling, why you think your connection would be strengthened by non-monogamy, and what ideas you have about how to incorporate those ideas into your romantic life together.

Some important things to not only think about, but actually discuss with your heart-person, are whether it's okay to see other people more than once, and in what context (Can you go on dates? Are you cool with only one-time, strictly physical encounters?), whether there's a limit to what you can do with your side-pieces (maybe kissing is totally peachy by you, but sexing other people is more of a moldy, rotten banana that you'll break up with someone for eating?), and how cool you are with telling each other about your external entanglements.

Be respectful: Trying to force someone to relax their boundaries is gonna end in tears. Locate a happy medium and stick to it. You love this person, so don't do things you know will hurt them. There's no simpler or truer aspect of romantic love than that one, for real.

Important side note! Non-monogamy doesn't necessarily mean you're having full-on SEX with strangers (or whomever else you're seeing on the side). Even if you're not having sex yet, you might want to kiss other people, or go on occasional dates, while still considering yourself half of a couple. This is doable, so long as you and your partner set ground rules early on. For me, non-monogamy is more about circumventing a general discomfort I have with being told not to do something—the classic reverse psychology of "I didn't want this thing until you told me I couldn't have it!"—than it is about getting down with some new person every night of the week.

The number one tenet of my own non-monoggo relationship with Wes was: *Don't tell me anything unless I ask—but be honest if I do.* Like, let's say I spent a day on my luxury yacht, the *Amy Rows-Your-Boat-Ashore*, with my two biggest celebrity crushes, Martha Stewart and Tupac, and after a few glasses of rosé, things got frisky and we had a three-way makeout (this is just a hypothetical and not a true story, so DROP THOSE PENS, *Us Weekly*!). The next day, if I were hanging out with Wes, and he asked, "So, did you get with anyone last night?" not even maritime law would exempt me from telling him the truth about this stuff, so I would say yes. Either he would be satisfied with that answer and move on, or, if he felt jealous and would rather know the reality of what happened than let his mind start spinning out paranoid fantasies, he might want to know more. If he asked for additional information, I'd answer him factually, but only to the extent to which I felt comfortable: I usually drew the line at describing nuanced details of physical encounters or identifying characteristics of the person (or celebrity businesswoman-rapper duo) I was fooling around with, for the sake of both our brains. While some people are cool with spilling everything about whose hands were on which deck, Wes and I knew we weren't okay with hearing all the salty details, and we respected each other's limitations.

That last thing didn't come up much, though: Wes and I didn't frequently ask each other, "Well, WHO WAS IT you were all up on, huh?" It was largely irrelevant, because our number two rule was: *Don't get with anyone I know or am likely to meet at some point.* We didn't want to run the risk of bumping into each other's sides of fries for reasons that had as much to do with manners as they did with wanting to avoid stoking jealousy—for the most part, I wasn't trying to make polite small talk with someone my person had recently gotten with. This wasn't because I wished that person ill; it was more that it was awkward for everyone, especially for the fries-piece to my romantic cheeseburger of a self, because they'd likely have been wondering if I *knew*, and *oh my god this is so uncomfortable ugghhhh.*

Our final rule: *Involve yourself with other people only when we're not physically available to each other.* If I felt like Wes was prioritizing spending time with someone else instead of me, I would be devastated and probably key his car, and he told me he would have felt the same if the sheets were swapped (and if I had a driver's license, which I don't). Luckily, when we were together, we felt a thermonuclear infatuation toward each other that made that potential difficulty and automotive disfigurement a non-issue.

• **Accept jealousy as an intractable factable of life.** From time to time, when an acquaintance of mine or Wes's saw me macking on someone other than my boyfriend or overheard me waxing feverish about some new person, they'd look confused. When I explained my romantical arrangement, they almost always gasped, "I can't believe you don't get jealous!" But it's like, YO, OF COURSE I DO, ARE YOU KIDDING ME? I am one of the most jealous broads on the planet, if I let myself be!

In some of the "monogamous" relationships of my way-younger past, I got paranoid every time one of my boyfriends went out without me. Since I was a cheater, I suspected that everyone else was, too. Even though I knew on an intellectual level that I was being waaaaay too sensitive, I still did things like sulk if a partner and I were watching TV, a deodorant commercial came on, and I thought the girl in it was prettier than me, which, of course, was a totally valid and logical reason to give my mystified beloveds the silent treatment for the rest of whatever *South Park* episode we were probably watching at the time. I also remember, on one occasion, ripping up a drawing that a mutual female friend had done for a guy I dated and blaming it on "a dog" like an uncreative homework-hating second grader, despite the fact that it was in his car and neither of us had pets. I think, in my tall tale, the fictional canine was owned by an equally fictional neighbor who came over to talk while I was sitting in the passenger seat with the door open. You would think that a seasoned two-timer like me would have come up with a better lie! Of course, no one believed me, and it was real embarrassing. As you might guess, the people I dated were also not too into my paranoid policing of their every movement.

Thankfully, I outgrew this jealous-fugue period after my first few relationships, when I realized the extent to which it made everyone, including me, miserable. Every now and then, though, I still feel a diluted version of the self-doubt that incited it. As you probably know firsthand, a large part of being a person, especially a female one, is trying to squelch the feeling that you're not attractive enough, or smart enough, or otherwise worthy enough of love. Even on my best days, these doubts skulk through my head and refuse to stop poking and prodding at the things I dislike most about myself, and so I project them onto other people—usually the ones I'm in relationships with, because when I'm in love with a person, I consider them the next-closest thing to myself in some ways, and therefore the most obvious recipients of these self-based hatreds. When I'm feeling shitty about my writing, or I suspect I cut my hair too short (ugh, it's more than just a suspicion, I know I totally did), those insecurities feed my fear that NO ONE COULD EVER LOVE ME and OF COURSE MY PERSON SECRETLY WANTS A MUCH MORE INTELLIGENT AND/OR LONGER-HAIRED GIRLFRIEND.

Here's the lovely thing about non-monogamy: Having realized that my issues have far more to do with my own brain than with what my partner chooses to do with his D, it was actually the hugest relief to me that, on the surface, the reality of my relationship with Wes (he and I slept with other people) was the exact worst-case scenario I would have imagined in my previous history of loving people. The difference is that back then, these dalliances would have been hidden and clandestine, and if I had found out about them on my own, they would have broken my heart (and then I would break everything my partner ever found comfort or enjoyment in) (maybe); whereas in my non-monoggo pairing, I was secure in the knowledge that none of that affected how massively in love we were with each other. Instead of feeling cataclysmic, sex was—whoa, it was *great*, and if I ever felt jealous, we just talked about it. I no longer let it melt my brain into a rage-magma that overwhelmed all my rationality, empathy, and happiness. Basically, not being pressured to stay sexually faithful to the person I'm committed to drove home the point that boning ≠ love, even though they obviously involve each other quite deeply in most relationships (including mine with Wes). This, in turn, helped me mentally redistribute my self-worth so that I don't freak out quite as much about increasing the amount of my hair/advanced degrees in comparative literature.

• **If you're having sex with more than one person, BE SAFE.** I mean, be safe no matter what kind of sex you're having with anybody, but if you have multiple partners, USE CONDOMS AND/OR OTHER BARRIER METHODS OF PROTECTION AND COMMON SENSE 357 percent of the time, with everybody, including your foremost paramour. I cannot stress this enough. Putting your partner's sexual health at risk is not only inconsiderate, it can be harmful to them in the long run. So please make a custom of being extra-safe.

• **Be fair to the people you're seeing outside the relationship.** I feel like all the best romantic wisdom comes from down-home country and blues singers, so here is a mournful old-timey ballad that I just wrote about telling a potential hookup that you're seriously involved with someone else (imagine that I am casually holding a banjo but not really knowing what to do with it and also I tried to put spurs on my Keds):

> *Tell them as soon as you can without presuming*
> *That something's gonna happen with your mouths or other*
> *   parts*

But definitely before getting physical or going on like twelve dates
And breaking their doggone heartsssssss

Wow. That definitely sounded like the kind of time-tested pro-
fundity that can come only from living off the land and your own
salty tears and probably there's a pickup truck involved. I reckon
(okay, I promise this stops here) that you should do what my awesome song tells you, partner (sorry, this really is the last time for
real) (more like sexual partner!!! ha-ha) (please don't go).

Obviously, this doesn't matter as much for one-time flings. If
you go skin-to-skin with a girl you meet on vacation or at a party
out of town, you don't need to recite your autobiography before
getting down to biz. But if you're more socially connected to a
person, or intend to see them more than once, the time to let them
know is as soon as possible. Some people you might want to mess
around with are not going to be receptive to the idea that they're
one of the many ships in your various ports, especially when one
of those is a yacht (I'm talking about your main squeeze, not the
old *Amy Rows*, here). Don't try to wheedle anybody into changing their mind. Not everyone is going to have the same attitude
toward casual hookups as you do, and that's their prerogative.

Some people might think you're lying about being non-
monogamous to try to get them to help you cheat. (The unfortunate reason for this is that there are horrible deceitful dicks in
this world who do exactly that.) It helps to disclose the realities of
your relationship clearly as soon as it feels like something's gonna
happen between you. The longer you keep it a secret, the more
it'll seem like you're being deceptive, because why would you not
mention it if you're not doing anything wrong? You don't have to
give them the WHOLE ENTIRE HISTORY of your relationship
and the philosophical reasoning behind your non-monogamy, as
I have here! Just say that you're in an open relationship—even if
you don't like the term, this is the easiest and most direct way to
get your point across. Then, if you want, answer any questions
they may have about it—although some people are gonna be like,

"GREAT, crystal clear on this one, let's make it happen," in my experience, they are in the minority.

• **Be prepared to be criticized.** Can I be honest with you for a moment? (Because everything I wrote before this sentence was a series of CRAFTY LIES, PRANKED YA, LIKING SEX IS ACTUALLY BAD!) Even though I'm comfortable with my decisions, I was nervous about admitting to having had non-monogamous relationships, because there is still a giant stigma attached to being a youngish female person who is not willing to conceal the fact that she likes sex and all its related behavioral trappings.

The criticism often comes in the form of slut-shaming, which sounds like: "How could you do that to him/her?" or "If you really loved each other, you'd be faithful," or the more concise "Don't you feel like a slut?" which I almost admire for its frankness, except I don't, at all. The implication behind all these comments is that it's "natural" if men want to sleep around, but when (young) women do, it's seen as self-serving and immoral. And you know what? I would like to politely invite such naysayers to go suck an egg, as long as we're in the business of telling people what they can and can't put their mouths on. Even if you find the idea of opening your own relationship abhorrent, it's shitty manners to treat those who choose non-monogamy for themselves like they're BAD or WRONG—both of which I can totally be at times, but never for this reason.

A less damning, but still undermining, backhanded compliment that people sometimes give me is: "Wow, I guess you're more *evolved* than I am—I could never do that." It's one thing to ask questions or be curious about non-monogamy, but entirely another to make a flat one-to-one comparison between two unrelated personal preferences about love. It makes me a little bit sad when people treat the private decisions that I've made like a critique of their own lives and relationships. My response is usually to say, "Nah, different people are comfortable with different things." People are not Pokémon—non-monoggo-hood isn't something you "level up" to when you free yourself from society's shackles, man. It's a personal choice about what makes you happy, and it's not for everyone!

The key to maintaining a healthy outlook about non-monogamy is not letting other people's dumb attitudes about it impact your mindset, so I deal with the aforementioned situations mostly by not worrying about them too much. They're so far from the reality of my life that I don't feel the need to explain myself—why bother clearing my name of some made-up wrongdoing I don't even believe in? It's the same as if someone came up to me and said, "How dare you steal the president's most beloved gold-plated Furby from the White House!" It's like, (a) that's not a real thing; (b) even if it were, I didn't. I just realized that that nonsense-scenario is a totally solid analogy for this whole conceit: The president is a primary partner, the gilded Furby is my vag, and the White House is the patriarchy's insistence that I live chastely instead of expressing what I want in a way that makes me happy. Excuse me while I go write twelve scholarly feminist texts based on this premise. Maybe I am an academic sex hottie after all?

All told, the only advice you absolutely need to follow when you're figuring out your own relationship configuration is to always be aware and considerate of your own and your partner's feelings. Keep talking! Do a State of the Union every so often to make sure you're both still feeling happy and loved, and if one of you isn't for whatever reason, make some adjustments and see if things improve. All relationships require communication and a genuine desire to be sweet and kind to the person you're dating. Hold these things at the forefront of your mind when you're deciding if you want to open your relationship. If you both decide you do, go get it, and above all, have fun and be respectful of the people you care about. That part'll come real easy.

PART III

Mistakes Were Made

I am loath to take part in the narrative trope that conveys, "Young women who have sex, in doing so, are embarking on a wacky, embarrassing, ill-thought-out comedy of errors," without some recognition of how cool and worthwhile casual sex can be. Sexual autonomy is often presented as "confessional"—either overly comic or overly melodramatic, and when a female sexual youth is described as a series of "misadventures," it rankles me. Upon taking in movies, magazines, and the anecdotes of others about the so-called bad behavior of a wayward woman they know, I so often feel like screaming, "She didn't lampoon or victimize herself—*she fucked someone!*"

I have never once seen a young dude subjected to the same hand-wringing or false pity that his female counterparts are so regularly met with, or a guy who, in every other beat of his story about a physical encounter, feels the need to giggle or apologize it into an acceptable shape for his listeners. If a woman has had sex that she likes: Enough with the jokey contrition. Sex doesn't have to be "bad" to be good.

Just as destructive would be recounting a sexual past that's been edited and finessed into a montage of soft-focus orgasms in which I am played by a young Natalie Wood, except with butt implants. I can't pretend that all the sex I've had was that of a swanlike pinup sans an overbite that makes head risky if I'm not careful. Making mistakes is one of my very favorite things in this life, because then you become aware of how they were forged, and how to avoid them in the future. The key is not letting them define, discount, or dissuade you from the superb aspects of your sex life, or even seeing them as extricable from those. Fucking up is how you go pro. No need to be abashed or apologetic about that.

When it comes to escaping most perplexing quagmires of sexual propriety, like how to contend with unexpected bodily effluvia, noises, behaviors, and getting caught masturbating by your roommate's new girlfriend Marie (sorry, Marie—this Hitachi is truly thunderous and I didn't hear you come in), act under one law: Instead of bugging out about your OWN potential humiliation and what this means about your sexual aptitude/worthiness, think about how to put the other person at ease about what is, in the grand context of life, history, and space, a nothing-event that you will have mostly forgotten about in a few weeks expeditiously. What is the gallant thing to do? Communicating that sense of calm and contextual awareness to your intended! Preserving your sense of personal security and confidence is easy when you consider that blights on what really should have resembled *swan-sex enjoyed by fat-butted movie starlets on le Francebeach* are also enjoyed by those same people, who are, by the way, fictitious.

If someone shames you for any natural/unexpected/otherwise potentially mortifying phenomenon occurring from what you're doing together, kick them to the curb with no compunction: Basic self-worth demands that you shouldn't be made to feel guilty if the sex you're having results in unwieldy bodily goings-on. No by-product of sex is repulsive enough to negate the commodities it manufactures: recreational sweetness and connection. And orgasms.

If you find yourself *actually* hurt or otherwise medically dented-up by any kind of sexual contact, locate real medical care. Though you can pull a mental assist using the following list of what to do should your *pride* be jeopardized, it does *not* stand in for a health professional. That said, here's everything you shouldn't be embarrassed about.

Queefing

Queefing is the colloquial name for the sound vaginas expel when vacuoles of air are trapped in them and then come out. This usually happens when something is inserted into them, and the likelihood increases if that something is coming from an unusual angle or at a variegated speed. Queefs are normal and inevitable when you're having interesting vaginal sex, and should be seen as a casual confirmation of that, not a ghastly interruption—or even something worth commenting on at all. Doing so is like admitting, "I have limited experience with etiquette." Some alternate lines of thinking include...

If you're the queefer: *Oh, a sound happened. Who cares?*

If you're the bequeefed: *Oh, a sound happened. Who cares? You do!*

Take it as a compliment. To the untrained ear, queefs might not seem harmoanius with the sighs of pleasure you're more used to classifying as evidence that your work is appreciated, but if you're smart, you'll come to hear these as hot.

Caught in the Act

If you live with people other than the ones you're having sex with, they're liable to know more of the intricacies of your goings-on than you'd both prefer, and vice versa. However vigilant you *think* you're being, there's always room for surprises here (especially if there's a meager amount of *actual* room in your home): It's possible you'll be caught in some compromising situation.

There are plenty of settings in which you can be witnessed in flagrante delicto. Public sex is the best precisely because of the risk of getting caught...until the rare occasion on which that risk is realized. And if you escape this life without someone interrupting you as you jerk off, it should go in your obituary with the rest of your notable achievements.

You could be apprehended in one of these ways when you

think no one else is home…and are dead wrong. Or maybe you and your partner are staying in a foreign living space with others for a big event, like a wedding, family reunion, or competitive spell-a-thon, got a little drunk after, and badly misjudged the window of private time you'd have back at the base. In any case: You've been caught, and your face is mad red. Regain your composure and maybe even, if you're a halfway decent actor, pass off your indelicate intertwining as a more chaste entanglement by…

• Considering your setting: Is it totally "inappropriate" for you to be boning in this context? Do you know you might harsh someone else's good time (e.g., are you at a christening or something?). Then maybe don't take off your clothes, or do so only with extreme caution. I don't think it's always bad to have sex in places you shouldn't, as that will probably make for some of the most memorable sex of your life, but draw the line at having it somewhere that's actively disrespectful to others (most of the time).

• Consider your potential audience: If you find you're not hurting anyone by being a brazen public-sex-having menace (e.g., a national park ranger is not going to be galled to the gills that you've deigned to desecrate a redwood with your grapplings— *something no one has ever, ever done before*). Many other non-forester people in non-woodland surroundings, if they have senses of humor, will laugh this off, and some might even be like, "Good for you—get yours." That leans heavily on the age and relationship factors in play here: Your mom, unless she is simultaneously unshakably cool and kind of alarming, boundary-wise, will not duck out like "Soz!" and then text you for the blow-by-blow later on, whereas your best friend might be more inclined in this way.

• Above all else, try lying: You don't have to be an actor of Nude-Brando proportions, but you do have to put on a little show about what it was you were doing that was *very much not sex*, no way, no how. No one WANTS to go through the excruciating conversation about the fact that they recently saw someone's butt for all it truly was. Do you know how badly the interloper is probably wishing you'll fill out the tail end of the phony statement, "We were just..." rather than having to accept the reality that they were watching you get some? Lying is the stepladder out of any potential sinkhole of embarrassment on the culprit's end, sure, but it's also a relief on the other end. Blaming clothing-related mishaps helps with any apparent nakedness: You were fixing a broken button on your partner's pants! They noticed your zipper was broken, and knew they had to step in to help! You were cleaning spilled punch off of their bra with your tongue! That is all VERY believable, as long as everyone is uncomfortable enough.

Premature Ejaculation

I have never understood the impulse to knock a premature ejaculatore, but I do get it! From what I've noticed, no guy wants to be remembered as the one who couldn't last—the loveless phrase "two-pump chump," which was popular among my high school girlfriends, whooshes to mind. Much like dudes who aren't hung, these people will usually put extra muscle into making sure you feel amazing with other parts of their anatomies. This is great news if you don't get off on penetration alone—so, this is great news for many, many people. If someone is looking to reframe how you characterize them sexually, they probably know the sure-fire way to go about doing that: giving you life-changing head.

Not Enough Lube/Not Fitting

I once had sex with a person whose genitalia fit so poorly into mine that getting him in me was like trying to hammer a bent-up screw into a sugar doughnut. I had no idea why this could be, or that it could even happen!

We were frustrated because we had been involved in a dire mutual crush for two years or so, and having gotten out of a relationship about five minutes (fine, five days) beforehand, I summoned him to hang (fine, nail/screw/otherwise misapply hardware euphemisms to me).

Even those you foster titanic infatuations with can be subject to compatibility-based bodily oddities. We tried all kinds of different positions and spit-based lubrications to try to make it work, which, eventually, it KIND of did? Instead of the natural pulse of intercourse it felt like... scraping?

Neither of us came, I don't think, and after getting home, I discovered that one of my labia was swollen. I did what I always do in times of medical crisis: avoided googling my symptoms at all costs—the pictures are life-threateningly gross and misleading; I have found 100 percent of the time I don't follow this rule. Instead, I dialed up my sage older sister, Laura, who is a lot smarter than I am, and less of a sensitive little nightmare who thinks she's dying or else STI'ed up because of benign swelling.

"I used a condom!" I wailed, sans salutation of any kind when Laura picked up, because I have excellent phone etiquette. She didn't balk, but calmly asked what happened, because *she* is the best and instantaneously gets it most, if not all, of the time. "I finally got it in with Alan and one side of my vagina looks like someone took a bike pump to it."

"Oh, dude, calm down. That's totally normal! Did you use enough lube?" I recalled that our only kind was salivary, and she told me to go sit on some ice for an hour. Post-deflation, I called her back to say thank you, having sufficiently calmed down enough to even say "hello" first. Since then, I make sure that if I'm carrying a condom, I've also got one of those single-use packets of lube close at hand, lest I run into another issue with my and a partner's construction.

Passing Gas During Oral

One of my best friends recently told me that her most bloodcurdling fear is "letting out a fart with someone's face in my minge."

Thank her home country of Britain for that delightful locution, and thank me for telling you that however homicidal this potential humiliation might feel, you are going to be fine—and your stomach, at least, will feel better?

Let's not minge words: This can happen, and while you should do your best to prevent it at all costs via the motivation of "basic human decency and respect," bodies are villainous machines that process their exports at uncontrollable clips sometimes. While I have never been either the deliverer or recipient of this wildly unpleasant-seeming olfactory tour de farts, I have been the unlucky, unwitting recipient of other gruesome anatomical products. And I am alive, and pretty much fine, if tinged crimson about committing this particular prose to the corridors of the Library of Congress.

You might not know how to slow things down gracefully, but you HAVE to, no matter if it looks peculiar, and then get the heck out of that room for a second. If you can't bring yourself to say, "Sorry, this feels amazing, but I need a moment," and repair to the john because you think it'll look SO OBVIOUS that you have a body that occasionally does normal bodily things, come up with an excuse. Say, "This feels amazing, but I got an eyelash in my eye and I need to get it out," then hit the bathroom, run some water, and come back saying, "Sorry about that—I feel way better now," and meaning it.

Period Blood All over the Bed

Did you bleed on someone's bed, or have a bloodletting on your own sheets? No big deal (unless maybe it's coming from someplace other than a vagina, out of a wound). Like most natural fluids, period blood doesn't have to stain your bedclothes permanently. If you know you'll be engaging in period sex, you can avoid any trouble here by laying out a burner sheet—this can be any old bedding or towel that you're okay with Jackson Pollock–ing with menses. If you discover that you or your partner is beginning their cycle immediately after you've finished in bed: Rush some seltzer onto the hemogravy in question.

You know how I can't seem to stop stanning for seltzer throughout this book, to the point that it almost reads as though I'm an infamously raunchy heiress to the Schweppes fortune? (GOD, I wish that were my life.) That's because you can harness the powers of carbonated water not only to keep your mouth pleasantly wet during oral and seeming like the kind of "together" adult for whom even WATER can be improved upon, but also to get blood out of fabric.

You don't want your partner to think you're grossed out, in large part because *you're not*, so don't act like you're trying to douse a wildfire. Calmly be all, "They're just sheets!" omitting any portion of that sentence in which you are tempted to enumerate the thread count of said bedclothes, and pour half a glass of the cold seltzer sitting on your nightstand. If this seems like an excessive amount of water: You want to keep enjoying that jacked-up number of threads, am I correct? Gently blot out the stain with paper towels. *They're just sheets*—stain-free sheets on which you also got to enjoy the miracles of period sex.

Condiment Attack

The most painful thing that ever happened to my vagina was when a boyfriend added "ZEST" and "SPICE" to our sex life in a tragically straightforward sense. We had been revising a new recipe for wing sauce to exactitude every few days for one whole summer, so it was a shame that I utterly lost my appetite for it when, after dinner, Chris touched me without washing his hands. We had forgotten that pepper hurts body parts other than just your tongue, and wing-based pleasure morphed instantly into intense pain. Even as I was wincing and screaming "THIS IS NOT WHAT 'HOT SEX' IS SUPPOSED TO MEAN, YOU JAG" at Chris, I was laughing and grateful to have a new story to tell my friends for the month, but since then, I have taken care to avoid buffalo-style sex.

Handling spicy foods like peppers—or wing sauce—before handling another person's D or V is the living worst. Wash your hands eleven times if you think you're going to bone after dinner, and maybe decide against cooking/eating scorch-inducing foods on a date. (And not only because they often incorporate beans, putting you at risk of "letting out" my British friend's gaseous terror.) If you still *heat things up* in the most regrettable possible way, get in a cold shower immediately, wing sauce be damned to burn on the stove in retribution for how it burned me. Flush out the point of contact, then take a break from sex until the next day. If you don't feel better in two hours, call a doctor.

Getting Come in Your Eye

I wear lots of makeup. As such, I'm far from intimidated by the prospect of effluvia around my general eye area. As with mascara, though, the key is making sure your optic nerves aren't suddenly clouded with alien liquids by applying them to your face with precision.

Did you know that when you see the world through a filter of semen, your eyes inflate and redden until they resemble rubber grade-school kickballs? If you're masturbating and have a curved dick, or if you're in the mood for a 100 percent natural facial treatment, consider your or your partner's aim.

I was given this unfortunate education recently, when I found myself looking down the barrel of a partner's loaded dick. "Wait—!" I yelp-cooed, trying to preserve both my fake eyelashes and the sensuous tone of klymaxxx, to no avail on both counts. My vision blurred with come. I brushed my tear ducts gently with the back of my hand as the dude susurrated apologies: He had never done this before! He lost control! He was so so so so sorry! I played it cool: It had come from his body, so it couldn't hurt me too badly, right? There was no need to jet off to the bathroom and flush my eyes immediately, as far as I was concerned.

That turned out to be wrong—semen does not make for a good saline solution *at all*. The swelling was swift and stung badly... and I had a meeting to go to in an hour. How do you even lie about such a highly visible vision-based irritation? I had no idea, as I'm an unskilled liar with an overactive imagination, but not a useful one. I came up with a bee sting to the eye, an allergic reaction to eyedrops on just the one half of my face, and, "Oh, this remedial sports equipment I'm calling part of my head? I was crying! I was crying very hard about... having... sadness," which doesn't work if you're trying to maintain a professional profile, but which I thought might still be better than the obvious conclusion of semen-eye. In the end, I canceled the meeting.

If this happens to you: Don't make my mistake of trying to be *all casual* about things. There's come in your eye! Get thee to a faucet and wash it out with water immediately! If, like me, you do not actually have an allergy to eyedrops, employ those afterward. Make sure your eye is totally cleansed of all semen—leaving any behind will be sure to irritate it.

Excrement

Obviously, I have little timidity about working blue when it comes to sex—which makes it all the more ludicrous and prissy that, when it comes to talking about scatological, urine-based, or otherwise execrable topics, I blanch—a lot. (See how, there, I had to use the most distancing possible language because I'm too prim to say the word "shit" in the context of bodily functions? Do you know how irrationally peevish I am that I just did? THIS IS A TOTALLY SCATOLOGICAL TURN OF EVENTS, for me.)

I am very selective about bodily fluids, sexually—except that one time that a boyfriend and I got uncharacteristically stoned, my home-for-once roommate was in the bathroom, and I really had to go. The solution we came up with, geniuses that we were, was that he could try drinking my pee. I remember laughing a lot and him saying, "It tastes like warm tea" and thinking, *Why wouldn't you just say "tea"?* before deciding the phrase "warm tea" was a very tender way to describe the taste of your loved one's piss in your mouth. That was a nice time. I never, ever want to repeat the experience, ever. (Unless, of course, I'm stoned again and the urge to urinate is outlasted by the duration of someone else's shower. Thank God I smoke pot roughly once every bi-never.)

Another thing I never want to do again: It took one new-at-the-time boyfriend, Graham, a while to feel comfortable in what he felt were esoteric new positions, like anything approaching the non-horizontal and firmly face-forward. One night, a lapse in his demureness involving a new rearrangement of positioning (prostrate; prostate) surprised me. At the time, I thought the most abhorrent interior design of our Holiday Inn room was a painting of a pond in which the lilies were literally gilded. I stared at it, lying on my stomach, as I linked its subject to the idea of having anal sex versus vaginal. I scoffed at myself and got back to enjoying the grip of the very specific pleasure-pain that comes only with taking it up the ass. I looked at the sheets after. Behold: *Nightmare.*

I bugged out and covered the bed, dashing to the bathroom, scarlet all over. Graham was immaculately gracious; he knocked on the door of the bathroom as I showered in scalding water and my own woe: "Take all the time you need—but, look, it makes sense that this happened, given what we were doing, and I'm not grossed out at all." I had to concede his point. I walked outside in a towel, evading his face for entirely different reasons than I had moments before.

The lily had been not only un-gilded, for sure, but left to rot in a compost heap. He tried to salvage what he could of my pride. "I don't think you're gross," he continued, and the precision of his kindness there is as follows: He knew there was no persuading me the situation wasn't objectively putrid, but he wanted to convey that he still liked me and didn't want me to seethe inwardly over an inadvertent by-product of having great sex, which is to say, the occasional *Nightmare.* Sweetly, he got to assuage MY anxieties about something that was, in essence, a microscopic (if colonoscopic) deal.

See how even the most self-aggrandizingly "open-minded" sex-havers can find, to their grim surprise, that maybe they're not as cool and carefree about the smashing together of anatomies as they envisioned themselves? This is why, when you shack up (or Holiday Inn up) with a slow-mover like Graham, it's crucial to be kind, patient, and uncondescending. Your partner might, after all, end up as gallant as you had always prided yourself on being when you find, instead, that you've shit the bed.

The Case for Celibacy

Sometimes, I don't have any room for sex in my life, and my body and brain decide to give me some space back. This has happened to me on a few occasions when I was focused on special professional projects (usually, I do both with relish, but on exceedingly rare occasions, I do one or neither for a while), went on a kind of anti-depressant that lessened my libido, and, at other times, I just didn't care to fuck anybody for a minute. When I've lost the signal for sexual frequency, in terms of both my erotic brain-buzzings and the rapidity with which I broadcast them outward, I have learned that it's best to not freak out and think, *I hate sex now forever, I guess???!!!* which would be fine but has never, historically, been the case. (Although wouldn't it be kind of hilarious if this book came out and then I got me to a nunnery?) When I do that, I'm berating myself for something I have found is ultimately instead kind of a sexual boon, and always a mental one. I am talking about a labial lie-low, the denial of all things penile, an extended hormonal holiday—whatever your anatomy, you'll be able to recognize it: the classic boning breather known (by me) as the Celibration.

I have a Celibration when I'm approaching the limit of having "too much" sex. Overdoing it has nothing to do with some ratcheted-up naked-body-count. It stems from the perpetually reshuffling alignment of variables like my self-esteem (am I having sex to feel good about myself, even once? that's too much sex); time (is my work lagging because I'm busy being a slag? sexcess); and scarcity of people I desire (every time I've had sex with a person from my hometown = critical-mass overload of sex, with the additionally injurious scents of hair gel and shame overlaying my over-laying). The bottom-line question: Do I straight-up *not want to* right now, "reason" or not? Then I'm on break. If the thought of sex bares itself in a way I don't feel is good news for my overall life zone, it's Celibration time.

This has meant lots of things for me in the past: periods of full-blown sexual abstinence, meaning NO DATES, NO KISSING, NO MASTURBATION, EVEN, as well as conversations amounting to, "Oral only—I'm taking the L on taking the D," with one of my long-term partners of yore. (We broke up for unrelated reasons long after my sex-break broke, before you ask, and he was cool about it—if he hadn't been, we'd have split for *highly* related reasons, namely that I don't ever want to be with someone who takes access to my body for granted.)

The first time I came down with a persistent case of celibacy, I tried to fight it. I was like a mulish office cold sufferer insisting she's just fine, saying *of course I can work*, as sodden tissues explode from her pockets and her eyelids hover at sunset-horizon-level. Is that person likely to nail a big account capably, given that her head feels like the contents of her overtaxed nostrils and she's not giving herself time to let it pass? No, and I was even less likely of capable nailing during that bout of sexual indifference and all the ones that followed.

In that case, I was twenty-one and had just completed my customary three-week, post-ruinous-breakup seminar on how to bone people who aren't actively in love with me, which is a bit what I imagine an extended continental vacation (a real one, this time) feels like. By the end, the novelty wears off, just as it's intended to: Three weeks is time enough to tire of your trip abroad, which is a necessary part of returning to the normal keel of your life without constantly being all wistful, like, *Man, wish I were in perfect old France right now. Fuck this apartment—there aren't even croque madames at any of the restaurants in my neighborhood.* Similarly, it's the exact right duration of time for noticing, *Huh—why is it that I'm not actively salivating over this obviously gorgeous person in my bed? Oh, right. It's because it has been my singular myopic focus to do just that, with as many people as possible, for the same amount of time that it would take me to complete an accredited Harvard extension class called "Gene Expression: A Hands-on Approach"; I miss edifying myself about more than just other people's bods...and I also haven't checked to see if my apartment is still there, for that matter, and isn't rent due pretty soon?* Congrads!! Now that you've relegated sex back to the equivocal plane of all the other lovely ways to spend your time, it doesn't seem so intimidating. When I do this, I am reminded that there's no such thing as being "rusty," which can bear repeating after long-term monogamous sex.

Flicking through my sex-based mental archives (i.e., spank bank), when I finally made it back to my (intact) apartment that time around, I realized it had been a full two and a half years since I had gone without sex for longer than a week running, and I wondered how it might feel to be a single adult who was not seeking out all-new ways to come as one of her more robust priorities. This was a region uncharted in my life, at that point. I had always had boyfriends and girlfriends, or else was rejoicing that I didn't and bopping around with others for whom that was also true. I decided to put my education to the test and explore the farthest-flung reaches of celibacy I could: *I nobly abstained from sex for an entire two weeks.* And it didn't even kill me that hard.

This first Celibration meant: no dates, no flirting, no contact, no Hitachi Magic Wand or other fantastic onanistics. I still went out alone or with non-beaus a lot, but I felt domesticated at first, like a dog tag–collared timber wolf glowering at the invisible electric fence in the front yard of a condominium, except hornier. I was my own captor—I wanted to gnaw my own arm off rather than hold out and suffer, but I also wanted to clock what happened when I quarantined the sometimes-rabid species of my own desire and watch how it behaved. I thought about sex a lot, but in the way that I think about going to the beach when it's cold out: *It's going to get hot again, and I'll be drunk on light beer for some of it. It never really goes away completely.*

I found that it agreed with me to live in a world of which sex was a faint, unobtrusive part, like the sound of cars that you can't see passing outside an open bedroom window. Both are greatly beneficial to my productivity: I am able to maintain the soft-edged awareness that life's transportational difference is just outside, but also that I don't have to witness those adventures firsthand *that very second* if I'm content to sharpen the blades of my own restorative privacy by reading, or figuring out how to build a shelf for my microscope, or lugging a bottle of vodka into my bathroom and taping fake hair onto my head for three hours, aka "drunxtendoing," or writing letters to my friends. The promise is still there, waiting to be kept whenever I'm ready to keep it. Not all favors are sexual. Sometimes they're ones you're content to do for yourself.

Taking a break from sex doesn't irrevocably strip you of the ability to be sexual. (In fact, it doesn't strip you at all.) Celibrations are worthy endeavors because not only do you discover how kind you can be to yourself, by yourself, but they also have the funny effect of making (s)external largesse seem like even *more* deliberate and mutual acts of generosity.

On Sluts

The Bylaws of a Very Noble Political Cause: Skank Advocacy

Credit: Esme Blegvad

(continued)

- Bicameral system of legislature? Please. It's the new times, these days. More like *bisexual system. Hell Yea.*
- We're bringing back the monarchy. Prince is our ruler now, so everyone stop voting. It's not like that does anything anyway. God
- Pick up a paintbrush because 1600 Pennsylvania is about to get purple as fuck
- Affordable school lunches for kids
- The national bird is a water bed now

I do not believe that the quantity of sexual partners a person has, or the frequency with which a person takes different partners, hollows out the sacral nature of sex. I was nineteen the first time I had sex with three different people in a day. This felt adventuresome in the way of a scavenger hunt: What new experiences could I collect in the given timespan? (1. *Make out with a Rolling Stones mouth tattoo on a dude's bicep.* Check!) God, it wasn't even that deliberate. I just happened to find myself in bed accompanied by three different partners, eyes open to eyes closed. (*I just happened to find myself* having triple-sex by seeking it out and being wild into it. So funny how these totally serendipitous coincidences work!!)

The first was Ahmed, whose bed was puffed, perfectly white, and unfamiliar, like one at a slightly upscale chain hotel—maybe a Hilton Garden Inn? I woke, turned to kiss him, and then rotated him on top of me as he whispered kind things about my body. We had been seeing each other for a few weeks. I felt like he was impermanent—like a person-shaped continental getaway, just as I did the rest of the cabal of people I had been dating and sleeping with following my first real trial of a breakup, with Chris. Ahmed liked to go to raves, which augmented this feeling. So did the fact that he was a breed of babe with an unclassifiable eye color—Pantone would drool over the challenge. His physicality was all-over compact, save for his aquiline nose, which jutted from him in the way that gorgeous natural landmarks invade their surroundings: a mountain on a plain; that one tree in the neighborhood with the knothole you hold weirdly dear. I ran one hand along his chest and trailed the other across his neck as he came. I didn't, but I would later. Exchanging the courtesies expected of us in this generic-hospitality setting, I affirmed that we'd had a blast, rescued my T-shirt from where I'd flung it into a corner, and dipped into the June air, feeling mad good.

My own bed belonged more in a dorm room than a Hilton, which was appropriate, as it was, in fact, college-housing-issued. Will didn't mind since he shared my age and unfamiliarity with upper-middle bedding—the first time we had sex was in his basement room at his parents' house in Park Slope, just after he cooked me a steak with a cherry-balsamic reduction, counted the swans that still lived in Prospect Park's gummy waters before the city's animal control murked them out two years later, and showed me his handgun. Besides owning an automatic weapon, another of his flavored boasts was that his grandfather was a famous American poet, whose writing I found bland in a patriotic O-the-snow-and-waterfowl-of-this-nation way. Outside of noting the seabirds, Will hadn't taken up the family trade, preferring instead to pursue the bifurcated career of model/Golden Gloves boxing champion/preschool teacher. He sang me Johnny Cash songs, described me as "a piece of candy" (I found this somehow charming?), and daydreamed about chartering a helicopter to show off Manhattan to me from where we could see it all at once. Unfortunately, he was also chokingly vain and sometimes used baby talk, which, against all likelihood, did not dissuade me.

When I called Will to come over on Three-D-Day, he was at my building in Brooklyn Heights within twenty minutes. I answered the door naked, hoping it'd expedite one more commonality we could enjoy on our other, aka my lumpen single-wide mattress. He peeled off his black henley. He was my height plus half, and—shocker—built like a Golden Gloves boxing champion. I loved looking at his legs, but avoided eye contact with his inflated biceps, since his fanged 40 Licks tattoo took up most of one of them. He smoothed my legs together over my torso and fucked me seriously and hard, like he was training. I came almost immediately, and he followed my lead there, too.

I told him I had a lot to do and would see him later. He left me grinning and perspiring, sitting cross-legged in the buff on my sheets, snorting the open-window perfume of a fresh day. My roommate unlocked our bedroom door not three minutes after he had maneuvered it closed with a combat boot behind him. "Hey?" she asked, used to catching me naked a bit later in the evening. "Hi! Oh. Chris just left," I explained absently, since she knew I was still seeing my ex and I didn't feel like telenovela-ing my situation to the person with whom I lived. "Oh, cool," she said vacantly, lighting a joint—I honestly don't know why I thought she or ANYONE would look at my sex life with consternation, or any opinion at all. I got dressed and opened a book, whiling away some time before "still seeing my ex" was expressed more honestly a few hours later.

Chris picked me up on the sidewalk and we stole into a diner and ordered hamburgers on English muffins (an ancient aphrodisiac, so I have heard, or would like to pretend I have heard). We hated being broken up almost as much as we hated being a couple, so we agreed to reinstate the mock-casual rituals of preliminary dating, when you don't know someone yet, so are able to make yourself sick gorging on your crush on them. We dutifully visited parks and photographed each other among their blossoms, plus ate at places with homey linoleum-paved tables, like this one, the location of which made it convenient to hop right back up to the room my roommate had vacated some hours earlier. Chris, like Ahmed, was wiry and avian-boned, but tall, and the nice thing about going on these impostor first dates with him was that, after, we got to skip the tentative nametag–style HELLO MY BODY IS introductory sex, since we'd already been fucking for two years. All of the excitement, none of the awkwardness, I'd say if I didn't think those two things were inextricable. I didn't think of Will or Ahmed while I was with Chris, but I was flimsily aware of their participation in the memory this day would become underneath the moment unfolding, in which Chris had his palms on my lower back.

Until now, I have kept all of this a secret. It's one-eighth because I wanted this private in-joke stashed where I exclusively could enjoy it, but I know the other majority of my brain concealed it because I didn't want to feel horrible about it—a realization that, upon having it the day after, *totally made me feel horrible about it*. Up until that point, I had had some, but not much, casual sex, and even though this seemed totally quotidian as it was happening, the network of other people's potential reactions kept me clammed up about it. I imagined being told, "YOU'RE BRAGGING," and, "YOU'RE OUT OF CONTROL," which are two of the main fears I harbor in all areas of my life, by anyone to whom I might have mentioned the triptych of different bedspread patterns I saw on my bed crawl.

I had had a great time and hadn't hurt anyone—I was, of course of course, as safe as one can be while having sex, and not one of my partners was in love with me to a degree that knowledge of my travails would have thrashed inside their brain or heart with any great agitation. Still, I thought that if anyone found out, I was sunk. I knew that nothing about this weighted or negated my ability to be kind to the people I held close, do well in my academic life or at my job, or think critically and write well. I just didn't think the rest of the world would know it, too, and so I felt imperiled by the idea of someone misunderstanding me based on that day's tally marks in my diary. I thought anyone's finding out would herald a life-sized crisis.

Maybe it will. Writ large, that has been my fear throughout writing this entire book, but I believe in it too much to care. I hadn't yet figured out back when, but no one who's living a fulfilling and generous life (same thing) gives a rat's ass about what other people want to do in bed. They'd rather not hear it, most of the time. It's so strange—the twin pinnates of this fear that, by relating my sexual autobiographies honestly, I will be seen as boastful while simultaneously also contemptible. Together, this duo is the great oxymoron comprising how plenty of people categorize those who have a lot of sex. The eternal rule of life is that no one sees you as you see yourself unless you make them. Stop forcing how you feel down their throats. If you think that you're an undesirable and are intent on letting other people know that, their initial impression of you as a potential font of mutual orgasms is compromised, and then you're sunk.

Not to be totally fucking gross and disgusting, but bonobos, our closest living relatives, are constantly on the move from one partner to the next. (They also live in a matriarchal society, which makes me think that bonobos may have their shit together better than we do across the board.)

People can fulfill all different sexual wants or quotas for you. I'm queer, so it's hard for me to not tomcat around like the blond Don Juan I am. Since I think having sex with people of all genders is kind of where the fuck it's at, it naturally follows that I prefer to do that! I also accept that it shape-shifts: I am currently seeing a heterosexual man with whom I want to be monogamous, and I allow that to be exactly what it is without bucking my diehard belief in the nobility of Skank Advocacy. I'm absolutely here for the cause even if I'm disinclined, at the moment, to hopscotch along the campaign trail. Not that this was ever my main motivation, or even a motivation, but my monogamous relationship benefits from my past canvassing, too.

That's because sleeping around had first improved me, the individual person. (This blandishment = present among all relationship advice, I know. But, like many things served plain, it's better for you than it tastes.) The more people you have sex with, the more fluent you are in all kinds of . . . tongues . . . when it comes to sexual communication. (Sex, as we know, is nothing if not communication.) You learn a language better by going to the country, as opposed to doing Rosetta Stone in your room. (Wait, I should have called this book *The Rosetta Bone*. Fuck.) This isn't to say that you can't explore yourself with a single partner—just that it broadens and expedites your education.

Having sex or its related acts with many people allows you to become the sovereign of your own sexuality, in part because you get to know your consistencies. What do you like across the board? I found it illuminating when I noticed that, whether I was in the company of a soft-spoken not-so-straight girl named Katie, my second male ex-fiancé, or that guy in the Hüsker Dü shirt that I picked up at Palace Fried, I adored getting head while I lay flat on my stomach. The ways each slept with me were specifically their own, but the basic procedurals were uniform—and uniformly rad.

What you'll learn extends to finessing your sexual restrictions as much as it does your WYLD FREAQ-KINKS: As all people have sexual idiosyncrasies that are worth salivating over, many of these also have not always had sex-related experiences that've been kind or respectful. (I call them "sex-related" because rape, assault, and other types of sexual violence are not also "violent sex." The first ordering of those words is the correct one.)

Perhaps you're uneasy, like I was, that should it somehow be made public, your affiliation with the Skank Party—or is it Party Skank?—will find you disinvited from the socials you had previously caucused for with other like-minded Sex Americans. That talking about it vanishes it. After thinking hard about this, I am no longer worried that the people I want to bone will turn up their noses at my contemptible whore's flesh. That sleeping with people has rendered me all-too-clearly SO repugnant that no one would EVER want to be with me. That logic bulldozes itself: People wouldn't want to fuck me because people want to fuck me? *Right...I see, Professor Heinrich J. Philosophy. Hey, do another one of your funny shadow puppets!!*

Having an abundance of sexual encounters for a certain period of your life doesn't make you "easy," since it's not like you've instated some policy of, "YEP, EVERYONE GETS TO SEX ME UP! THE RUMORS ARE TRUE! SO MANY RUMORS, AND THEY'RE ALL VALID!" It doesn't have to say ANYTHING about how you think of yourself—unless you'd like it to, despite the shadow-puppetry you might encounter to the contrary.

I'm not pressed about being criticized by would-be bed

notches. If a hypothetical bedfellow DOES lose interest in or esteem for me because of my Lifestyle-clad lyfestyle choicezzzz, I am grateful that they have given me the cue to follow suit. (The only times, for me, that I can simultaneously agree *and* disagree with a person are in moments like these. If anything, rather than getting offended by the few instances when this has happened, I kind of relished them for that teleological weirdness.)

My only anxieties about the people concentric to my partners and me: In what ways could my *bad behavior* make someone else unhappy? Would the mutual acquaintances my partner also dated resent me? Would they go sullen if I walked into a room or, God forbid, SPOKE to their now-steady boy/girlfriend? Would it mean that my family would be disappointed in me, should they happen to google my name and find either the copse of essays I've published about RUTTIN' 'N' SLUTTIN' or the photo series of me ass-naked in a heart-shaped Jacuzzi, covered in McDonald's cheeseburgers? (As you witnessed in an earlier chapter, I happen to love fine art and totally cotton to what venerated critic John Berger says about the depiction of women in artwork in *Ways of Seeing*: "Men look at women. Women look at themselves covered in fast food and get totally jazzed that they ever not only had, but executed, that clever idea.") Or perhaps they would be disappointed by this very book in your hands? Would they, if not disown me, dispatch throat-clearing noises and half-joke-half-dig comments about my "...er [achhhhacchhhhachh]...free spirit" at family potlucks? (Open letter to each and every one of my uncles: I exhort you to just smile and pass the condiments without any wacky wordplay, however hilarious-seeming it may be, when it comes to this work of literature.) Would my friends decide I was that dreaded combo—boastful; shameful—and leave me if I ever let on how much I loved the D (and V)? *God, why did everyone have to care so much about my sex life???*

Of course, in reality, they don't. As with my gloriously indifferent stoner roommate of yore, I have come to find that no one gives a dollar-menu burger about what I do in the buff. It's funny to me that I could ever think that the people who love me would perma-seal the doors to their hearts because I take part in an activity that many, if not most, adults enjoy. There are few reasons for your own dear people to have to find out about and/or discuss your love life in the first place, so QUIT FREAKING OUT ABOUT IT, if you are.

In the case of a person's new partner with whom you're social: Take heart. I had sex with a friend of mine for a summer. His current long-term girlfriend was pretty out on me at first, as I think they started seeing each other right at the tail end of the sexual part of my friendship with him. I was disappointed by that, but I understood. I had been curt to women who made me feel weird about the people I loved before, and so I also knew how they made me feel better, which was treating me like any other regular stiff whom they were happy to be pleasant to and bro down with. They made themselves *people* to me instead of *sex avatars that were undermining my relationship*, and so I follow that same method.

As far as your friends are concerned: Why is it that you're so much more willing to take their version of THE RIGHT THING TO DO seriously than you are your own? You've got more self-possession than that, I hope, whether you're having an orgy with your whole apartment building or zero people at all. If your friends scoff or condescend to you re: your sex life, either stop talking to them about it or stop talking to them full-stop. There's a reason Blanche is the best Golden Girl (and if you try to contest that a priori fact, there's no talking to you in the first place).

The only potential difficulty here is based in how "sluttiness" is gendered—there CAN be real-life consequences, and more harrowing ones at that, for women and queer people to a greater degree than for men (although men are not totally exempt). But that doesn't have to stop anyone. If it did, we'd be missing out on so much.

As I noted earlier, the best sex I've ever had was with a (sort of) one-night stand—Brafe, the longhair I plucked off the sidewalk. We had sex in the darkness of his apartment without talking. As

I leaned back into the quiet island of his bed and he fucked me with his feet on the floor and his knees on the sheets, the silence and skill of it redefined what sex was, and could be, in my life. It exemplified another funny and perfect element of sex: Once the cosign has been given, consent-wise, talking can feel like you're interrupting a conversation in which you're saying what you intended to speak aloud, but get across more cogently with your body. There are some things you can only learn through touching another person. If I weren't willing to sleep around, I wouldn't know that.

Being a slut, or whatever your characterization of being a sexual innovator is, is making a commitment to observe, french, and in all ways, touch as much of life as possible. You can do that alone, or you can do it with a cavalcade of exquisitely strange others. However you invent your sex life, you will find that like all kinds of affection, it's emulous—it expands. The more of other people's intimate and nuanced approaches to sexuality that you try to understand, accept, and welcome, the more of that generosity you can then pass on to the rest of the world with respect, bravery, extraordinarily messed-up pillow hair. Most of all: with love. Do with that what you will.

Further Resources

Fetish Resources, by Which I Don't Mean "Porn":

Kinsey Confidential, which has all sorts of resources and articles on freaky sex pour vous: http://kinseyconfidential.org/category/pleasure-orgasm-posts/

Edukink http://www.edukink.org/articles/

Clarisse Thorn http://clarissethorn.com/bdsm-resources/

The Kink Aware Professional Dictonary https://ncsfreedom.org/resources/kink-aware-professionals-directory/kap-directory-homepage.html

Lingerie:

True&Co

Frederick's

Agent Provocateur

Sex Stores:

Babeland
http://www.babeland.com
Good Vibrations
http://www.goodvibes.com
The Pleasure Chest
http://thepleasurechest.com
Dr. Shanna Katz's list of sex-positive brick-and-mortars throughout America: http://shannakatz.com/links/sex-positive-toy-stores/

Acknowledgments

My endless gratitude, esteem, and so forth is the permanent property of the following beloveds: Rookie, who supported and generated this book in manifold ways; soup dumplings; Ma, Lito, Laurg, Maddy, and our family as a collective—forever and ever, and for everything; Dimitri Stathas aka DVS par excellence, who sat up with me through the night and rubbed oil on my mitt during the entire summer I spent writing my proposal; Dan Kirschen, my agent extraordinaire; Libby Burton who edited me gently and strongly; Charles Aaron; Tavi Queen Gevinson, who is the aperture through which this exists; Lena Queen Singer for extending me her signature grace and camaraderie—and more or less making it possible for me to finish this; Lauren Redding, the team captain; Action Park; Joseph Mitchell; Julianne Escobedo Shepherd; John McElwee; everyone I've ever fucked; everyone in general; Hermione Hoby for friendship and being one of my two readers; Rosie Lichter-Marck for the same; every editor I've ever had, but especially and above all, Anaheed Alani; ROOKIE ROOKIE ROOKIE and all of its people; www.rookiemag.com, in case that wasn't yet clear; Laia Garcia; Jake Fogelnest, who said, "You'll be amazed at what can happen if you just FINISH THE THING" and was right; Caryn Ganz; E. B. White, whose essays I read once or more a day before starting; Wayne Koestenbaum for the same; Jesse Miller-Gordon, my research assistant and love; Maggie Thrash, who kept saying, "Tell me the first word of your book. Or the last one"; Meredith Graves; Jessica "Jayhawk" Hopper; Sonja

Midboe; Helen Gurley Brown; Sarah Nicole Prickett; Andy Ward; Andy Kaufman; Morrissey; The Jane Hotel and my own lunatic impulses (also, everyone who visited me at Gitane—JMG, Bree ["goodbye, f-friend!"], JES, SNP, Ganzy and John and Tavi, who came without a word of hello and contributed more work to the air); Brafe; The Paris Suites Motel's fake plants and view of the Unisphere; G. I. Gurdjieff; Stephanie Kuehnert Lewis; Lucy Betz; Annie Mok; Esme Blegvad; Gabby Noone and Hazel Cills; Steve Gevinson; Buffy Sainte-Marie; Matt Groening; Nick Brown; Lulu Penny; "Greenies"; Taha, I know this reads like I'm signing a yearbook and I don't care, God, seriously. (Also: God. Seriously!)

Index

Accessories. *See* Sex toys; Vibrators
ADHD, 24, 26
Alcohol
   consent and, 5–6
   in profile pictures, 56
   for threesomes, 165
Altruism, 35–36
Anal stimulation, 114–16
Animals, in profile pictures, 56
Apollinaire, Guillaume, 159
Asexual, defined, xiv
Asking questions, 40–42, 158
Ass play, 114–16
Augustine, Saint, xi, xii

Babies, in profile pictures, 57
Ball gags, 149
Barrier method. *See also* Condoms
   and sexual consent, 11
BDSM, 139
   resources, 207
   sex toys for, 149–50
Becoming yourself. *See* Sexiness-
   inducing life rules
Bedroom
   in profile pictures, 56
   serving breakfast in the morning,
     77–78
   setting the mood, 74–75

   tidiness and cleanliness, 71–74
   welcome home, 68–71
Beliefs, figuring out, 25–26
Ben wa balls, 149
Berger, John, *Ways of Seeing,* 204
Beyoncé, 30
"Bisexual" and sexual orientation,
   16–18
Bleeding, on the bed, 187–88
Blindfolds, 150
Blow jobs, 102–3
   how to give, 108–13
Bodily well-being, 26–27
   cautionary measures, 89–90
   masturbation for, 35
Body confidence, 64–65
Body weight, 67–68
Bondage tape, 150
Bonobos, 202
Bookstores, for meeting people, 47
Boundary setting, 95–99
Bowie, David, 19–20
"Boy About Town" (song), 16, 17
Brafe, 48–49, 205–6
Breakfast, serving in the morning,
   77–78

Camcorders, for porn, 133–34
Carrey, Jim, 119

Celibacy, 193–96
Cell phones
    for making porn, 134
    ungluing yourself from, 33
Charles, Ray, 26
Cheating, 166–67, 170–72
Cis/cisgender, defined, xiv
Cleanliness, 56, 71–74
Clinton, Bill, 23–24
Coital conversation, 119–23
Cologne, 74
Community involvement, 32–33
Compliments, 29, 41, 50, 58
Concerts, for meeting people, 50
Condoms, 83–86, 175
    breaking, 85
    sexual consent and, 11
    stocking up on, 84
Consensual sex, 3–12
    different scenarios, 4–6, 92
    first tenet of, 8–9
    how to grant, 9–11
    physical health and, 11
    setting boundaries, 95–99
Contraception. *See also* Condoms
    emergency, 85–86
    sexual consent and, 11
Conversations. *See also*
    Introductions
    asking questions, 40–42
    listening closely, 24–25
    making eye contact, 23–24
Coworkers, sex with, 41–42, 51–52
Crops, 149
Cruising, 16
Curiosity about a person, 40–42

Deep-throating, 112
Dildos, 148, 152
Dirty sex talk, 119–23
DIY porn, 130–34
Dominator, in BDSM, 139
Douching, 66

Eating pussy, 102–3
    how to, 105–7
Edible panties, 146
Ejaculation
    in the eyes, 189–90
    premature, 185
Emergency contraception, 85–86
Employment. *See* Work
Endorphins, and masturbation,
    34–35
Eros, 15
Ethical smut, 127–29
Excrement, 190–92
Eye contact, 23–24
    during blow jobs, 108–9
    cruising, 16
    winking, 38
Eyes, ejaculation in, 189–90

Farts (farting), 186–87
Feminine handjob (fingering), 103–5
Femininity, 14, 64
Fetishes, 134–40
    comfort revealing, 134–37
    professional sex workers for, 140
    resources, 207
    three extra-special, 138–39
Fifty Shades of Grey, 143
Fingering, 103–5
Fingernails, 61, 104
Flirting, 28–29
Focused attention, 24–25
Foods
    breakfast, serving in the
        morning, 77–78
    edible panties, 146
    seduction snacks, 78–79
    spicy, 188–89
Foucault, Michel, *The History of
    Sexuality,* 15
Frenching, 102
Freud, Sigmund, 15, 155
Friends (friendships), 28, 32–33

Gallop, Cindy, 129
Gardasil, 11
"Gay" and sexual orientation, 16–18
Gay male culture, *cruising,* 16
Gender identity, 13–15, 16–18
Gender pronouns, use of, xiv–xv
Gender-tangling, 138
Gender vs. biological sex, xvii
Gevinson, Tavi, 22*n*
Glossary of terms, xiv–xvii
Going down. *See* Oral sex
Good Person, 56–57
Grooming, 63–66, 73–74
Ground rules. *See also* Sexual consent
    setting for open relationships, 170–72
Group sex, 159–66
G-spot, 105
Guns, in profile pictures, 57

Handcuffs, 144, 149
Handguns, in profile pictures, 57
Handjobs
    female, fingering, 103–5
    male, how to give, 107–8
Healthy body, 26–27
    masturbation for, 35
Hemingway, Ernest, 65
Herpes, 88–89
Hide! That! Garbage!, 72–73
History of Sexuality, The (Foucault), 15
Hitachi Magic Wand, 145, 151, 153
Hogarth, William, 130
Holzer, Jenny, 83
Home. *See also* Bedroom
    setting the mood, 74–75
    tidiness and cleanliness, 56, 71–74
Home decor, 56, 68–71
Home security, 95

Hookups, 9–10, 43–44, 176
    spending the night together, 116–19
Hope Diamond, 21
HPV vaccine, 11
Hüsker Dü, 49, 203

ID Glide, 148
Illnesses, 27
In flagrante delicto, 183–84
"In Search of Duende" (Lorca), 77
Insecurities, 19–21, 64–65
Intergender couples, and threesomes, 164–66
Internet dating. *See* Online dating
Intimacy and Desire (Schnarch), 19
Introductions (introducing yourself), 38–43, 47–53
    asking questions, 40–42
    best spots for making, 47–51
    less-advisable spots for making, 51–52
    opening lines, 39–40

Jam, the (band), 16, 17
Jealousy, 173–75
Job. *See* Work
Jokes (joking), 20, 42, 58

Kindness, xi, xii
Kissing, 39, 102
K-Y Jelly, 147–48

"Life instinct," 15
Life rules. *See* Sexiness-inducing life rules
Likes and beliefs, figuring out, 25–26
Lingerie, 146–47
    resources, 207
Listening closely, 24–25
Lorca, Federico Garcia, 77
Lorde, Audre, 17

Love and sex, conflating, xi–xii
Love Boat, 18
Lubricants (lube), 147–48
  not using enough for sex, 185–86

MakeLoveNotPorn, 129
Masculinity, 14, 64
  anal stimulation, 114–15
Masquerading, 55
Masturbation, 34–35. *See also*
  Vibrators
McBeautiful, 39
Medical health, 26–27
  masturbation for, 35
Medical status, 11, 89
Meeting people. *See* Introductions
Menstruation, 187–88
Mental health, 26–27
"Mirroring," 65
Missed Connections, 54
Monogamy, 166–68
Mood, setting the, 74–75
Morning-after pills, 85–86
Morrissey pompadours, 61
Music concerts, for meeting
  people, 50

Narcissism, 20–21
Nicknames, 49
Noise, during sex, 112–13
Non-binary, 90
  defined, xiv

Onanism. *See* Masturbation
One-night stands. *See* Hookups
Online dating, 45–47, 52–58
  graciously turning someone
    down, 59
  masquerading, 55
  profile picture tips, 55–57
  writing and responding to
    messages, 57–58
Open relationships, 166–78

Opinions, figuring out your, 25–26
Oral sex, 102–3. *See also* Blow jobs;
  Eating pussy
  passing gas during, 186–87
"Orient yourself," 17

Paddles, 149
Panties, 74, 146–47
Paranoia, 173–74
Parties
  accepting invitations, 29
  for meeting people, 50–51
  throwing, 31–32
  treating life's offerings and tasks
    like, 36–37
Partner sex, 154–59
  adding a third person, 159–66
  feedback, 155–59
  open relationships, 166–78
Passing gas, 186–87
Perfume, 74
Period blood, on the bed, 187–88
Personal beliefs, figuring out, 25–26
Personal character, 20, 34
Personal hygiene, 63–66, 73–74
Personal insecurities, 19–21, 64–65
Personas, 30–31
Pets, in profile pictures, 56
Phones. *See* Cell phones
Physical health, 26–27
  masturbation for, 35
  sexual consent and, 11
Pickup lines, 39
Piss, 190–91
Planned Parenthood, 86–87
"Politically correct," 61
Politics, 25–26
Polyamory, 169–70
Porn, 125–27
  blow jobs in, 108–9, 111
  dirty talk in, 119–20
  do it yourself (DIY), 130–34
  the ethical smut, 127–29

healthy consumption of, 125–26
sending links to, 123–24
sexual "type" and, 60–61
Premature ejaculation, 185
Professional sex workers, 140
Profile pictures, 55–57
Progestin, 85–86
Pronouns, use of, xiv–xv
Pubic-hair grooming, 65–66
Public sex, 183–85
Public transport, for meeting
    people, 51

Queefing, 183
Queer, 18

Rabbit vibrators, 150
Rape, 6–7, 92–95
    defined, xv
Rape culture, defined, xv
Rape fantasy, 138–39
Reading series, 32
Rejection, 38, 44
*Remembrances of Bone Zones Past
    (RoBZP)*, 4–6
"Repressive hypothesis," 15
Resources, 207
Restaurants, for meeting people, 49
Restraints, 144, 149
Rookie, 22
Roommates, 71, 76
Rope, for sex, 149
RuPaul, 30

Safe sex, 175. *See also* Condoms
Safe space, 94–95
Salary talk, 13
Sasha Fierce, 30
Savage, Dan, 170
Saying yes. *See* Sexual consent
Schnarch, David, *Intimacy and
    Desire*, 19
Screen time, 33

"S Curve," 130–32
Seduction snacks, 78–79
Self-confidence, 19–20, 64–65
Self-esteem, 19–21, 193
Self-loathing, 27, 65
Self-possession, 19–22
Self-reinvention, 30
Self-righteousness, 56–57
Sensual touch (touching), 101
Setting boundaries, 95–99
Sex
    absurdity of rules on, xii–xiii
    conflating love and, xi–xii
    defined, xv–xvi
    vs. gender, xvii
Sex garments, 146–47, 155
    resources, 207
Sex industry, 128–29
Sexiness-inducing life rules, 23–37
    accepting invitations, 29
    becoming involved in your
        community, 32–33
    caring about your body, 26–27
    excelling at your job, 33–34
    figuring out your likes and
        beliefs, 25–26
    flirting with everyone, 28–29
    getting altruistic, 35–36
    going places you love by yourself,
        27–28
    listening closely, 24–25
    making eye contact, 23–24
    making friends of all stripes, 28
    masturbating, 34–35
    throwing parties, 31–32
    treating life's offerings and tasks
        like parties, 36–37
    ungluing from your cell phone, 33
Sex-positive, defined, xvi–xvii
"Sex-positive" porn sites, 129
Sex stores, 141–45
    resources, 207
Sex-symbolization, 19–20

Sex talk. *See* Talking about sex
Sex toys, 140, 144–50. *See also*
    Vibrators
  maintenance of, 152
  replacing, 153
Sexual assault, 6–7, 89–95
  cautionary tale, 90–91
  defined, xv
  safety and security tips, 93–95
  saying no, 92–93
Sexual autonomy, 13, 181
Sexual consent, 3–12
  different scenarios, 4–6, 92
  first tenet of, 8–9
  how to grant, 9–11
  physical health and, 11
  setting boundaries, 95–99
Sexual identities, 16–18
Sexual limitations, ideal time to
    discuss, 9–11
Sexually transmitted infections
    (STIs), 88–89
  testing for, 86–88
Sexual mistakes, 181–82
Sexual "orientation," 16–18
Sexual positions, 113
Sexual repression, 15
Sexual taboos, 15, 139
Sexual tension, 35, 101
Sexual "type," 60–61
Sex workers, 140
Showers (showering), 65
Shyness, 13–14, 41, 46, 136–37
Sidewalks, for meeting people,
    47–48
Silicone lubes, 148
Simpsons, The, 9
Skank Advocacy, 197–206
Sluts, 197–206
Slut-shaming, 177, 181
Small Deluxe, 30–31
Smartphones. *See* Cell phones

Snacks, 78–79
Sneezing fetish, 135–36
Spicy foods, 188–89
Spontaneity and sexual consent, 8
Stare-downs, 23–24
Stigmatization, 13, 86
STIs, 88–89
  testing for, 86–88
"Straight" and sexual orientation,
    16–18
Strap-on harnesses, 149
Stuff your life, 22
Submissive, in BDSM, 139
"Sup," 57
Swingers, 170

Taboos, 15, 139
Talking about sex, xiii, 15
  granting consent, 3–12
  limitations, 9–10
  with partner, 155–59
  talking dirty, 119–23
Testing for STIs, 86–88
"This Is Water" (Wallace), 36–37
Thomas, Dylan, 47
Threesomes, 159–66
Tinder, 52–53
Tongue
  blow jobs, 111–12
  eating pussy, 105–6
Touch (touching), 101
Toys. *See* Sex toys; Vibrators
Travel, 27–28
Two-person sex toys, 148

Underwear, 74. *See also* Panties

Vagina
  eating pussy, 102–3, 105–7
  fingering, 103–5
  G-spot, 105
  queefing, 183

Vaginal douches, 66
Vibrators, 144–45, 150–52
  maintenance of, 152
  replacing, 153
Volunteering, 35–36
Vonnegut, Kurt, 39

Wallace, David Foster, "This Is
    Water," 36–37
Ware, Chris, 21–22

Ways of Seeing (Berger), 204
"Welcome Home" parties, 32
Welles, Orson, 168
Whips, 149
Winking, 38
Work
  excelling at, 33–34
  friendships at, 32–33
  linking attraction and, 41–42,
    51–52

About the Author

Amy Rose Spiegel is a freelance writ(h)er and editor, most recently for *Rookie*. Her work has appeared in *Rolling Stone*, the *Guardian*, *NME*, *Dazed & Confused*, the *FADER*, *BuzzFeed*, and many other publications. She came up in New Jersey and currently lives in Brooklyn, New York.

Action : a book about sex

31290096175856   CA